Time on the Thames

ERIC DE MARÉ

Time on the Thames

SECOND EDITION

Flare Books

FLARE BOOKS
An imprint of The Harvester Press Limited
2 Stanford Terrace, Hassocks
Sussex, England

Time on the Thames
first published in 1952
by The Archictectural Press
This edition first published in 1975
by Flare Books, Hassocks, Sussex

'Time on the Thames'
© 1952,1975

ISBN 0 85527 072 1

Printed in Great Britain by Redwood Press Limited
Trowbridge, Wiltshire
Bound by Cedric Chivers Limited
Portway, Bath

New Preface

In spite of the changes brought by a quarter of a century, The Harvester Press has found it worth reprinting this book in facsimile. It was first published by The Architectural Press in 1952. Does it date? Far less, I gladly believe, than might be supposed, thanks largely to the building restrictions imposed both by floodlands and by the Thames Conservancy, and no doubt also by the river's many articulate protectors. Although the hope of designating the line of the tideless Thames a National Park has not yet been realised, modern depradation has nowhere badly debased the river's charms. It is, of course, far more crowded in summer than it was; remote serenity may be harder to find but the river's air of relaxed gaiety remains. Only here and there have the tree-murderers struck: a splendid old beech at Sonning lock has been cut down to make room for a squalid little pissoir; at Radcot Bridge two great poplars that once helped to form a "sweet, especial, rural scene" have vanished; no doubt many elms have died from the dreaded disease, while the bosky stupor that once ensconsed the Trout Inn above Oxford has been rudely broken by a concrete parking desert. The motor car has brought changes to the river in other parts too, not all of them objectionable; the new road bridges that cross the river near Staines, Maidenhead and Oxford are comely enough. That fine, wide view below Henley stretching to the far distance on either side of Temple Island remains bucolic while everywhere the colourful and variegated wonder of the trees can still be enjoyed to the full in spring and autumn.

At Marlow Lock the white timber mill has been replaced by a block of flats, but Tierney Clark's fine suspension bridge above has been saved and strengthened. That delightful long wooden bridge with its Japanese air that wanders out from the towpath to Marsh Lock, around the weir and back to the bank also remains to complete the most picturesque of river scenes. (Here I have discovered that the bridge was designed by Gainsborough's brother, rector of Henley).

Among regrets is the disappearance of that curious street of college barges along the meadow-side at Oxford, in spite of enthusiastic efforts to save them. Even if displaced a few of the barges have, in fact, been saved and refurbished, like the fine example, with its baroque carvings and "Victory" windows at its stern that once belonged to Jesus College and now lies in good state and in public use, above Maidenhead Bridge.

The statue of Father Thames reclining with a spade on his shoulder that came in 1958 from the Crystal Palace grounds to Thames Head was so mutilated by vandals that in 1974 it was moved after repair to St. John's Lock near Lechlade and replaced at Thames Head by a dull but indestructible block of granite.

A major change along the river is the replacement of manual labour by electric power in raising the paddles and opening and closing the gates at the locks. That eases the toil of the lock keepers, controls the waters more smoothly, and speeds the progress of craft, but something of the old *genius loci* of the upper Thames has thereby been lost: the convivial commune of the lock when by-standers would lend their backs to the gate beams and exercise their muscles at the paddle gears, as well as the visual effect of those immense levers of painted timber that projected from the gate tops. On the river, hurry should still be regarded as mortal sin.

On the whole changes have nowhere been devastating. A hope of construction lies in the re-opening of the Kennet and Avon Canal, whose slow resuscitation is now being undertaken by bands of dedicated volunteers; its opening will once more link the river most pleasantly with the west country. The Thames and Severn Canal remains utterly derelict without apparent hope of revival. But who knows? If the present discontents of life can be overcome and we can all work more for fun than for money, the rebuilding of long-lost amenities like this delectable road of water that once joined the two rivers through the Golden Valley, may become possible.

In a recent change in administration, the old Thames Conservancy Board has lost its authority to the Thames Water Authority. It has become a Division of the Authority but continues its benevolent work in the whole catchment area of the freshwater Thames. Within the Division is a Fisheries and Amenity Manager and staff covering the entire area of the TWA. Let us hope their eyes will watch protectively and that their activities in turn will be watched by vigilant local groups so that the vulnerable beauties of our unique linear park will be retained for posterity.

Additions have been made during the past quarter of a century to the literature of the river, among which the book I most readily recall is *The Thames* by a former Thames Conservator and riverside dweller, the late Sir Alan Herbert. I also recall quotations from the letters of William Morris that appear in Philip Henderson's biography of the great man describing two journeys he made up-stream from Hammersmith to Kelmscott in 1880 and 1881 — journeys that form the basis of the best chapters in *News from Nowhere.*

Not one year but twenty-five have passed since my wife and I explored the river in a floating box on one of those sunlit summers that seem to last forever. Still I have not made my second journey. My wife is dead, and I fear the poignancy of a return. I also dread to discover too many intrusions by this age of technological barbarism. That dread is no doubt unjustified; even since Morris rowed upstream with his jolly crew nearly a century ago the river scene has changed remarkably little — around Kelmscott hardly at all. The Stream of Pleasure, wandering down its green valley, continues to give comfort, for, to quote Jefferies, "that which flows continually by some sympathy is acceptable to the mind, as if thereby it realised its own existence without end."

Contents

Illustrations

ILLUSTRATIONS

Acknowledgements

All the photographs in this book were taken by the author except the following:—
P.20 foot, p.22 top, pp. 24-5, p.33 foot, p.34 top left and top right by H. de B. Galwey (The Architectural Press); p.43, by R. C. Gilliat (from *The Observer*); p.81 top right, p.86 top by Ian McCallum (The Architectural Press). Acknowledgements and thanks are also due to the following authors and to their publishers for permission to quote short passages as follows: to Marcus Whiffen and The Architectural Press (*The Architectural Review* May 1948); to Barbara Jones and The Architectural Press (*The Architectural Review* December 1948 and *The Unsophisticated Arts*); to Hilaire Belloc and J. M. Dent & Sons Ltd. (*The Historic Thames*); to Fred Thacker (*The Thames Highway*); to Dr. Tancred Borenius and the editor and publishers of *The Burlington Magazine*; to D. S. MacColl and Cassell & Co. Ltd. (*The Thames from Source to Sea*); to Negley Farson and Victor Gollancz (*Sons of Noah*); to Sacheverell Sitwell and B. T. Batsford & Co. Ltd. (*British Architects and Craftsmen*); to John Piper, John Betjeman and John Murray (*Murray's Berkshire Guide*); to the editor and publishers of *Punch* (The '*Lazy Minstrel*' poem). The author also wishes to thank all those river people, including those on the staff of the Thames Conservancy Board, who have given generous help and information.

E. de M.

Introduction

A GREAT MANY BOOKS have been written about the Thames. The Thames can stand yet another one because the subject is evergreen. Each generation sees the river differently, and, within a single generation, each individual sees it differently too and in a way that may be interesting and revealing to others.

A hundred years and more ago, Boydell, Ireland, Tombleson and Ackerman looked at the river with pleasure and recorded what they saw in their charming books of plates—plates made from copper, stone and steel. Today, as here, the photographic plate records the vision. The forms may be old but the vision is new because photography has taught us to look at things from a fresh and exciting angle.

The desire to undertake a journey and to point out the places of interest and beauty on the way is by no means new. It is probably as old as humanity—certainly as old as those early Thames topographers and their contemporary, the good Dr. Syntax, whose zeal for picturesque travel this author echoes thus:

> I'll make a TOUR—and then I'll WRITE IT.
> I'll *prose* it here, I'll *verse* it there,
> And *picturesque* it ev'ry where.
> I'll do what all have done before;
> I think I shall—and somewhat more.

The author has indeed made not one tour of the Stream of Pleasure but several, each time looking for something new in the sights of the river to record in his log or with his camera. Each journey has been an adventure of discovery. Now these discoveries are passed on to the reader in the hope that they will give him as much delight as they have given the author; that

13

when he ventures on the water at the week-end or during the summer holiday in punt, canoe, hired cruiser or river steamer, or picks up a rucksack and strides along the towpath (soon to become a continuous walk), his time may be the more enjoyable.

Facts of interest are recorded, facts collected first-hand on the author's own river journeys made in summer time, and second-hand on journeys made by the winter's fireside along the ever-flowing river of Thames literature.

We shall discover not just the well-known river monuments and features as we travel upstream, but the small and hitherto unrecognized things as well—the fine robust forms of the locks with their sturdy gates, their bollards and furniture set like pieces of modern sculpture in the ship-shape gardens—or the unpremeditated planting of the verdant trees which somehow always seem to fall into magnificent, informal compositions as though deliberately placed thus by some sensitive but powerful landscape painter—or those footbridges in their pale grey paint built by the anonymous engineers of the Thames Conservancy Board, which because they are small and made of wood and purely functional are rarely recognized as the fine little structural monuments they are.

No attempt is made here to repeat what Robert Gibbings has done so brilliantly in his discursive *Sweet Thames Run Softly*. This cobbler sticks severely to his last—things of interest and beauty to look out for, and to consider, on the Thames—even if that last is adaptable enough to shape such amorphous and unphotogenic objects as the river's ghosts and phantoms.

It is hoped that this book will be useful as a guide in three ways. First, the reader can glance through it at home to see if the river appeals enough to become next summer's choice for a holiday. Having decided that it is, he can, secondly, use the book to fix what reaches are likely to be most to his taste, for to discover the whole will need more than the conventional fortnight's leave. Thirdly, he can use the book as a reference during the voyage itself to help him select those places he finds may be most worth while visiting during the limited time available. For instance, he may reach Benson late one sultry afternoon. Shall he suffer a two mile walk 'inland' to see the old almshouses and monuments of Ewelme? Do the words and

In Ewelme Church: left, a corbel; right, part of a 1647 wall-monument.

pictures suggest that the place is really as entrancing as it is said to be? Or is a dip and a long, long drink more to be desired? The book may help him to decide.

But besides acting in this way as a guide to the visual pleasures of the river, the book has another object. The Thames may not be the grandest or the most beautiful river in the world, or, for that matter, in England. The Wye and the upper part of the Severn, for instance, offer finer scenery. But the non-tidal Thames (that is above Teddington) has qualities of its own, a special style that runs all the way from Teddington to Cricklade, a style that is unique but at the same time typically English. The Thames is, indeed, an open-air museum of English culture, history and tradition—a microcosm from which a general impression of the whole country can be gained.

Considering the besmirching of the landscape elsewhere by uncontrolled industrialism, and considering how densely populated are the areas of the south, the Thames has remained remarkably unspoiled. But time marches on and brings changes to the world and to the Thames. The danger is that these changes will be for the worse. We do not yet sufficiently appreciate our river and for that reason we are likely to permit its beauties to be spoiled more than they yet have been. The book's other purpose, therefore, is to help to increase the number of Thames lovers and, though dealing mainly with the past and the present, to act also to some extent as a guide to the future by pointing out what is most worth while preserving on the river and how, since some change is inevitable, the best of its traditional character can be retained and enhanced.

In a special issue of *The Architectural Review* on the Thames published in July, 1950, the author dealt with the proposal that the best way of preserving the river as a pleasure resort was to designate it as a National Park. There suggestions were made on how such a unique linear park could be treated. The pith of that argument is presented here during a spell of rest during our progress up-stream. Though discussing the Thames as it might become and not as it is, this section may be entertaining to the Thames traveller and encourage him, as he glides along in the present, to paint his own fantasies of the future just for the fun of it. This section, too, may not only help him to recognize the present virtues of one of our finest national heritages but will give this volume something which most guide books lack—a positive, constructive bias.

If the text of the book fails to stimulate, it is hoped that the pictures will do so and that the reader will at least accept this work with Sterne's brief comment: 'Give me a companion on my way, were it only to inform me how the shadows lengthen as the sun declines.'

Seen on the Thames, the carving on the rudder of a Dutch boat.

1

Panorama

BEFORE SETTING OFF, let us first soar high up above the the valley and take a heron's eye view of the whole—a panorama of this long, winding, domesticated snake as it glitters benignly along the borders of seven counties.

Between Teddington and Lechlade the tideless river winds for 135 miles. Yet all the way, with its towpath and enclosing belt, its width is only a few hundred yards at most. Nevertheless it can be regarded as a distinct region, almost a country on its own, for it has its own special character, pattern and traditions.

This character has been created partly by nature working on her own but mostly by man working with nature, because, however far back one looks through the centuries, the river seems always to have been under some degree of human control. It is essentially domesticated, tamed, artificial, as every point shows from the prehistoric earthworks on Sinodun Hill to the Home Guard's pill box on the bend at Kelmscott, from the ancient stone arches of Radcot Bridge to the modern concrete span above Iffley, from the great park of Nuneham Courtenay to the ten square yards of lawn and pergola at 'Beggar's Roost' or 'Wyworrie' which dip to the water at Penton Hook.

Apart from the drama of the chalk lands at Cliveden and the Goring Gap, its country is always quiet and modest, with its rich meadowland, its deciduous woods, its gentle hills and its tranquil, though never turgid, stream. Its homely villages, towns and structures, while being peculiar to the region, epitomize the history of England for, as Hilaire Belloc says: 'England has been built up upon the framework of her rivers, and, in that pattern, the principal line has been the line of the Thames.'

17

Except for the modern developments near London, at Reading and at Oxford, there exists no other thickly populated landscape in the country which has changed so little in its features as the Thames Valley. The whole is as arbitrary, informal, restrained, variegated, romantic and as shy of rigid trammels as the English character. It is the most English of English rivers and the most English of English regions. Yet as an entity it is unique.

What influences have created this peculiar and agreeable region, which has been for nearly a century the Thames of the pleasure boat, the public stream of pleasure?

Nature has provided the land formation. Above Oxford most of the valley forms part of the Vale of the White Horse—wide flood lands floored with clay, whose tame contours are relieved below New Bridge by the rag of the Berkshire Ridge with its dominating Wytham Hill. At Oxford an area of gravel rises only a few feet above the flood level. From Wallingford to Maidenhead the river crosses the chalk belt with its beech-covered downland and its swampy terrains. Here the finest scenery is found. Sometimes it even approaches grandeur—the twin mounds of Sinodun (which may at one time have stood out as islands in a great inland sea), the hill at Streatley (which rises above the gully where a few million years ago the Chilterns joined the Berkshire Downs), the lovely slopes of Hart's Wood, the steep declivity at Park Place and then the grand climax at Cliveden. From Maidenhead towards the sea come the more prosaic effects of gravel and clay, if we except Cooper's Hill rising behind Runnymede and the chalk bluff on which Windsor Castle stands.

On this geological basis humanity has formed the river pattern. Little is left now that is pre-medieval, for prehistoric man—the Celt, the Dane, the Roman and the Saxon—preferred the dry uplands for their lines of travel. Only in medieval times did the Thames become an important means of communication; the whole valley was, indeed, mainly the creation of the Middle Ages.

Above Oxford, though the river is now narrower and the land less marshy owing to land drainage, and excepting the modern locks and the heedless march of the pylons, the river has barely changed at all through the centuries. 'If a man wishes to re-

This first group of pictures are random ones to illustrate the distinctive
general character of the Thames above Teddington, the Thames of the
pleasure boat. ABOVE is the oldest bridge of the Thames, that at Radcot
on the upper river. Rich with the stone patina made by the weather of
seven hundred years, it is one of the many man-made adjuncts which
enhance the river landscape and help to make the Thames an open-air
museum of English culture, history and tradition.

B

TOP LEFT, a row of lombardy poplars, so typical of the river, stand along the tow-path in the Goring Gap, their rigid formality relieved by a break and the whole scene improved by a small timber footbridge. BELOW LEFT, one of the most charming landscapes of the Thames—the weir at Marlow, which echoes the curve of the suspension bridge and contrasts with the spire of the church. ABOVE, one of the spinneys, called the Wittenham Clumps, which top the twin hills of Sinodun; these hills, known locally either as the Berkshire Bubs, or, for reasons now forgotten, as Mother Dunch's Buttocks, dominate the landscape around Dorchester. BELOW, the small skew bridge above the rollers at Iffley Lock.

22

TOP LEFT, a rich treescape seen from Monkey Island gives that frequent Thames thrill of something exciting round the next bend. BELOW LEFT, a backwater at Benson where a distant lombardy, like a church spire, completes the picture. ABOVE, the old bridge at Godstow frames a view of Port Meadow and the distant spires of Oxford. BELOW, Medmenham Abbey, now a large country house, but once a cell for Cistercian monks. OVERLEAF, a river steamer, decorated with rows of lifebuoys and a white plume of smoke, churns past Henley towards the regatta reach to vanish in the haze of a June morning.

Milling has been one of the basic industries of the river for centuries. Many old mills still stand; a few still grind corn. ABOVE, the ancient abbey mill stream at Abingdon which runs by the ruins of what was once one of the greatest and proudest medieval establishments of the kingdom. ABOVE RIGHT, the white weather-boarded mill at Marlow Lock still serves a useful purpose. BELOW RIGHT, a modern paper mill at Sandford, one of the few industrial obtrusions of the river, now covers the site of a water mill which stood here at least as far back as the 13th century.

The river's economic life today largely depends on catering for leisure hours. LEFT, one of the many boatyards of the river where river craft are made and repaired. RIGHT, one of the Georgian inns of the river, the *Angel* at Henley. BELOW, a crowded river steamer approaches Boulter's Lock at Maidenhead on a sunny Sunday morning.

29

TOP LEFT, one of the best of the Thames railway bridges, otherwise rarely notable—that at Maidenhead designed by Brunel which has the two widest pure brick arches in the world. BELOW LEFT, fishing in the lasher at Goring. ABOVE, Romsey Lock is one of the typical Thames locks, which with their robust forms, fresh paint and ship-shape gardens, create much of the special Thames style.

Among the virtues of the Thames locks are their simple, economical, unselfconscious timber footbridges. ABOVE LEFT, the bridge over the rollers at Boveney Lock. BELOW, the bridge across the weir at Old Windsor Lock. Also decorating the locks are weir machinery, lockgates and such things as bollards, granite verges and steps, which, though made for practical use, act by accident as sculptural adornment. ABOVE RIGHT, the garden at Marsh Lock.

Though winding along the borders of seven counties, the Thames of the pleasure boat is like a distinct region and has produced a distinct riverside folk with their own ways of life. One of those ways is that of the lock-keeper who lives beside his lock in a well-built cottage and is king in his small, idyllic realm. ABOVE, the lock and cottage at Hurley. LEFT, three riverside types —an old ferryman at Molesey and two lock-keepers. Finally, in this river panorama come the trees. The trees *are* the Thames. They grow luxuriantly and form an aesthetic bond along the whole length of the river. LEFT, a lovely, casual treescape at Marsh Lock; the conifers are not characteristic but are perfect in this context.

33

Some more treescapes. ABOVE LEFT, near Cookham Dean is an arrangement punctuated by a tattered growth which somehow enhances the quality of the picture. ABOVE RIGHT, a less interesting scene in danger of breaking the characteristic informality of the Thames treescape. BELOW, an informal group of poplars, most typical of Thames trees, creates contorted reflections in a boat's wash along Henley's regatta reach.

capture a scene of the Middle Ages', writes John Buchan, 'there are two at hand to choose from. One is Merton Street in Oxford in a snowy winter twilight; the other is some stretch of the river in June above Godstow, where it twines brim-full, like a stream in a missal, with on each side miles of waving grasses, and in the distance a wild hillside and the spire of an ancient church. In such a landscape you can cheat the centuries, for all that is presented to your ear and eye is what medieval England heard and saw.'

Below Oxford some medieval marks still stand—defensive positions as at Wallingford and Windsor, the University of Oxford, monastic and conventual establishments as at Godstow, Bisham, Medmenham and, most powerful of all, the great Abingdon Abbey. All the convents are now in ruins and merely suggest how much the Thames lost at the Dissolution, for of the others—the Priories of Cricklade and Lechlade, the Abbeys of Eynsham, Rewley, Osney (with its fine bell-tower, seven storeys high and crowned with a spire), Streatley, Reading, Chertsey, Cholsey, the Nunneries of Burnham and Little Marlow, virtually nothing remains.

From Oxford down to Marlow the 18th century is still most in evidence, not only in the farming landscape which, as throughout England, is largely the creation of the revolutionary Enclosures Acts, but also in the many aristocratic mansions standing on the slopes and framed in their bosky parks—Nuneham Courtenay, Howbery, Mongewell, Basildon Park, Coombe Park, Harleyford Manor. The 18th century has given much also to the several pleasant riverside towns whose foundations go far back in time—least perhaps to Abingdon, that peer of Thames towns and, being still partly medieval, to Ruskin the most beautiful town in Europe; much more to Marlow, Henley, Wargrave, Sonning, Goring, Wallingford and Benson.

These towns have all borrowed something from each other, and yet remain individual. They have a quality of their own which distinguishes them from all other towns in the world. They are self-centred market towns, yet, on account of their commercial water-link in the past with the metropolis, possess a certain air of sophistication, and even today retain their urbane, Georgian character.

The 18th century has left many fine bridges, too (the finest, perhaps, is Swinford Bridge), and here and there a Roman temple or some little garden conceit peeping through the trees. That a great deal of this 18th-century and Georgian influence is left can be seen by comparing the actual river scenes of today with the engravings and aquatints of the topographical works of the 18th and early 19th centuries. If anything, the growth of trees since their time has often improved the landscape.

Though the river has been used to some extent as a pleasure resort for at least three hundred years, it remained right up to the early part of the 19th century the Silent Highway of London and during the Canal Era when the Oxford, the Grand Junction, the Thames and Severn and the Kennet and Avon Canals were built, the commercial traffic on the river must have been fairly heavy. Yet surprisingly little now remains to show the importance of the river either for commercial transport before the railways came, or for the other two main economic purposes— milling and fishing. The former importance of fishing for the Friday fare is remembered only in place names (such as the ubiquitous Fishery Row), and even the eel bucks, which our fathers saw, exist no more. Some mills remain, however; a few still grind corn and stand as pleasant features in the landscape with their square lanterns and white weather-boarded walls— as at Hambleden, Marlow Lock and Sonning.

The towpath is the most obvious relic of the days of commerce on the Upper Thames, and to the Linear National Park which is proposed in Chapter VII, it is of the first importance, as we shall see. Most of our rivers were without horse-towing paths till the early part of the last century and, before the continuous towpath came to the Thames, it was common to see a score of men hauling at a barge along the riverside meadows. The continuous Thames towpath is thus not very old and its useful service lasted only a few decades. Its present legal position is confused, and as a whole the public has no clear right to use it except for towing—a position which has to be cleared up before the proposed Riverside Walk is established.

Today the river above Teddington Lock—that part now administered by the Thames Conservancy Board—is essentially a pleasure resort, its chief economic purposes being to supply more than half of London's water supply and, of course, to assist in land drainage. Commercial transport is negligible, though even now a tug and barges can sometimes be seen as far up as Reading. Most traffic ends at Shepperton Lock, where it turns off onto the Wey, and the total merchandise carried in 1949 was a mere 281,000 tons, at least half of this being coal for the Kingston Power Station. As for the other economic purposes of the river, all come under the heading of catering for recreation and refreshment—the building, repairing and mooring of boats, cafés and inns, river steamers and fishing rights.

In the middle of the last century the Great Western Railway came to the Thames Valley. Its effects on the river scene have been considerable. The direct ones are the least and consist mainly of bridges across the river—Brunel's three noble brick aqueducts at Basildon, Moulsford and Maidenhead (the last with a fascinating echo and the two widest brick spans in the world) and the eight others which are not in the least noble (bright paint of good colour might help them). The indirect effects of the railway are profound, for this brought the river within reach of the whole London populace.

While bringing great changes, at the same time the railway helped to preserve the river character in that it stifled water transport and so kept industrial blight away from the banks, except at Staines, Oxford and Reading. Above Marlow the changes are less noticeable than below it, where the first innovations were the large Victorian mansions set in their dark, romantic gardens. The Gothic fantasy of Oakley Court below Bray and the castellated pile of Danesfield silhouetted against the sky on the hill above Hurley are typical. But such are few and the larger riverside houses belong to the Edwardian era of which typical examples stand most of the way between Bray and Marlow with their confusion of turrets, gables, verandahs, balconies, white fretted railings and barge boards, all set behind luxuriant gardens and ornamental boat-houses. Until the Wars and the tax gatherers brought the stealthy liquidation of their owners, they were always superbly maintained, but today too many show signs of neglect. Once we fumed at these fantasies, then we tolerated them, now we regard them with affection, sometimes even with respect (yes, even the Seven Deadly Sins above Pangbourne) and always with a certain, reactionary nostalgia for the departed Forsytean culture they express.

Steam-plus-petrol brought the bungalow suburbia of the

Little Man and this most affected the reaches below Staines. But this is far more pleasing than suburbia proper, partly because water, with its moving reflections, mitigates all ugliness and partly because many of these bungalows have a certain home-made charm. Far too many, of course, are merely squalid shacks (there is a bad outcrop by Walton Bridge), but many, as Miss Barbara Jones has described them*, are 'nautical and snug, shipshape dolls' houses',individualistic yet somehow homogeneous in their gay 'fluvial manner', with their jumble of small gables, long verandahs with white fretted railings—oriental, Art Nouveau, baroque and curly, plenty of fresh white paint, small sloping gardens ending in a drooping willow, whitened steps and verges and landing stages of infinite variety. All add to the pleasure and interest of a river journey. We should not scorn these amateur pieces of architecture for they are a kind of modern folk art, the crude and unselfconscious origins of a culture which limited spare time has nurtured and which only more and more spare time together with greater affluence can encourage and develop.

What other influences have been at work to create the visual character of the river? Among the most important is the benevolent one which the Thames Conservancy has exercised for nearly a century. The river has gained much by its charming locks, which, with their firm solid forms painted in the T.C. 'house colours' of white, pale grey and black, create such perfect foils to the foliage around them and provide such enjoyable interludes on a river journey. The Conservancy has developed an excellent vernacular style of its own with its roots in what has been called the Nautical Tradition of design—the simple, satisfying look of things you find wherever ships congregate. Most notable are the Conservancy's small engineering structures.

Some of the lock cottages are over a hundred years old and possess the pleasing patina and proportions of their age; others are relatively modern but they have always been designed with a certain care, and their gardens are beautifully kept by the lock-keepers, who are stimulated by annual competitions among themselves. Each lock-keeper has power in his small

* In *The Architectural Review*, Dec., 1948; subsequently reprinted in *The Unsophisticated Arts*, 1951: Architectural Press.

kingdom and gives to it something of his own personality. Thus every lock has its individual stamp but at the same time continues the universal, basic forms of granite edging, heavy timbered gates and beams, smoothly sculptured bollards and whitened steps.

Last but not least the trees. These grow luxuriantly and form an aesthetic bond along the whole length of the river. The trees, in fact, *are* the Thames. In the gardens, the weeping willow and the weeping beech, the acacia, the chestnut and the occasional cedar; in the countryside the common beech, the elm, the chestnut, the pollard willow, the black poplar (lovely when seen shimmering against blue sky) and, dominating all, the tall lombardy, especially telling when it forms a punctuation to the horizontal sweep of the river bank. These trees are never regularly disposed and it is their informality, the apparent naturalness of the planting which is so characteristic. Much of this treescape is the heirloom of the days when tree planting was considered the first of public virtues and when the eye had been trained by several generations of painters and writers to appreciate the picturesque view. The tradition, though sadly weakened, is with us still.

The Thames regional style, diverse yet unified, runs, then, all the way from Teddington to Lechlade and beyond. Yet the river can be divided into three distinct sub-regions. First comes the river suburbia up to Staines, less built-up and lined with more vegetation than one would suppose, for there are extensive open spaces at Hampton Court, Shepperton and Laleham. The suburban effects can be seen as far up as Marlow, the first real independent riverside town. Secondly comes the stretch from Staines to Oxford with its Home County look, containing the finest scenery of the river—the quintessence of the Thames. After the squalor of Oxford's back yard (which must be thanked to some extent for acting as a kind of protective barrier to the far solitude) comes the third sub-region, the Medieval Thames, which has already been described. Here industry obtrudes only in the form of a Victorian paper mill at Wolvercot, a sugar beet factory at Eynsham and a regrettable neo-Georgian waterworks at Swinford. Though scenically unexciting, the region has its own special charms which are at their best in the late spring when the river still runs high and 'the wide grass meadows that the sunshine fills' are green and succulent. Its remoteness and meandering tranquillity are its chief attractions and away above the floodlands lie many delightful villages with their ancient manor houses, inns and churches, most of which deserve a visit —Wytham, Cumnor, Stanton Harcourt, Appleton, Northmoor, Cote, Bampton, until at Kelmscott and Lechlade one is well inside the Cotswold country with its fine local stone. Above Kempsford come Castle Eaton and finally Cricklade, where the river becomes a mere trickle by mid-summer.

That inspired sociologist and freelance town planner, Sir Patrick Geddes, divided a distinct region into three basic elements—Folk, Work, Place. We have dealt with the Work and the Place of our strip region. What of the Folk who inhabit it— the third of Geddes's trinity? Something too has been said of them—of the floating population, the week-end and summer immigrants from the metropolis, the urban shuttlecocks seeking refreshment by the water. These, as we have seen, have contributed largely in their strange fashion to the Thames fabric. But what of the natives—those who live on and by the river— the lock-keepers, ferrymen, mill workers, inn keepers, villagers, tradesmen, riverside farmers, the few surviving toll-bridge keepers, and the men of the boat-yards? Do they make up a regional type? It is always dangerous to generalize, but roughly speaking they do. It is one which has been formed by intermarriage among the old river families, by climate, by the kinds of work the river produces which swing with the soothing rhythm of the seasons, and by the cheerful genius of the place. The type is physically well set up, parochial to the river, solemn, contemplative, quiet—sometimes almost to moroseness —but kindly and welcoming as the summer's flow; easy to rouse to a quick resentment as the winter's torrent. It is the air of languor which most marks it—like the languor of a slow punt in the brooding warmth of a summer's afternoon. The river seems always to be reflected in the eyes, flowing on smooth and endless. The type is in sharp contrast to that found on the estuarial river and at the port with its cosmopolitan, maritime alertness.

Proud of their riverside crafts, delighting in a well-turned-out boat and in the study and domination of the water, the men of the river scorn the clumsy, modern tyro; especially so the older ones, who remember the easy, shining days of the bourgeois river cult with its steam launches, parasols, ornamental house boats, the Three Men and champagne at Tagg's, when to embark on any sort of craft without white flannels and rubber-soled shoes was to be banned from Society as being 'not quite the clean potato', not of the 'real river people'.

To be one of the real river people in this more democratic day, it is enough that you should treat the river with the same deference and affection felt by Soames Forsyte when he reflected on his return to Mapledurham after a trip abroad: 'Have they such a river as the Thames anywhere out of England? Not they! Nothing that runs so clear and green and weedy, where you can sit in a punt and watch the cows, and those big elms, and the poplars. Nothing that is safe and quiet, where you call your soul your own and think of Constable and Mason and Walker.'

2

Teddington to Staines

YOU MAY NOT START your river trip from TEDDINGTON but
it is convenient to start this book from there for several reasons.
It is a main articulation of the river because it is at this point
that the Thames Conservancy takes over from the Port of
London Authority; here the proposed Riverside Walk to Cricklade will begin; here, discounting the special half-tide lock at
Richmond, is the first lock on the river (or, rather system of
locks, for there are three); here also, the last effects of the tides
are felt. Perhaps one should say 'nearly always felt', because at
certain spring tides it is possible to shoot the weir in a canoe
upstream, and it has been recorded that, during an exceptionally
high tide on 12 March, 1906, 'so full was the stream at Teddington that a tug was carried through the lock without the gates
being opened'.

Ireland in 1791 writes of Teddington: ' . . . formerly called
Tide-ending Town, from the tide, as it is said, having flowed so
high, before the building of London Bridge.' But that is absurd
because, before the first lock was built here in 1811, the tide
could be noticed as high up as Staines. An old spelling is
Todyngton—the settlement of the sons of Tod.

Teddington must have been a remote and rustic spot a
hundred years ago before the London sprawl encompassed it.
Then a writer noted that 'the air is pure and mild, and the
situation delightful . . . the fall of water over the weir has a very
pretty effect, being the best attempt at a cascade we know of
around the metropolis.' Yet the place still retains that charm
which water always gives even to the most squalid surroundings, and this first of the many sparkling weirs we shall pass still
makes a very pretty effect.

Of the town itself, which you will probably not explore for

At Teddington the Thames Conservancy Board takes over river control from the Port of London Authority; there the last effects of the tide are felt and there is the first lock. From Teddington, then, we begin our upstream journey, coming soon to Hampton Court Palace, our own homely, brick-work Versailles where, on the piers of the entrance, the Lion and the Unicorn stand for ever on guard.

43

LEFT, the towpath above Mole-sey Lock. BELOW, the genuine Swiss chalet at Hampton behind a thick cluster of moored pleasure craft. ABOVE RIGHT, the riverside park at Hampton facing Tagg's Island. BELOW RIGHT, the classic temple in the lower garden of Garrick's villa at Hampton; inside, in Garrick's day, stood a statue of Shakespeare which Roubiliac carved in the 1770's

LEFT, Pentonhook Lock cottage, one of the earliest on the Thames, built in 1814, and one of the best in design. BELOW, Sunbury seen across the weir stream with the 18th-century church tower and the riverside inn.

BELOW, the ferryman's Georgian cottage at Laleham.

you will be anxious to be on your way, it is enough to say that it is distinguished for having housed, in the 17th century, William Penn, founder of Pennsylvania; for containing the mortal remains of Richard Bentley, who helped Horace Walpole to design many of the details of Strawberry Hill, that first of the skin-deep Gothik Revival fantasies,* which lies a short way down stream; and for the church monument to Sir Orlando Bridgeman, the lord of the manor, who died in 1674. When the church was being overhauled in 1833, the vault was opened and there lay Sir Orlando embalmed and in a perfect state of preservation even to his pointed beard. The Earl of Bradford, his descendant, was immediately called and so had the eerie experience of gazing on the face of a progenitor dead for nearly 160 years.

Aboard now and into the foreign land of the river—foreign because once you embark on water, however narrow, you become at once detached in some strange way from the mundane world. That is why, even though at least as far as Staines we shall be passing through a built-up river suburbia, we shall not be bored or half as eager to reach the upper rusticity as we had anticipated. Even here we are explorers in a new land.

A short way up we pass Trowlock Island and, on our left, the new Kingston power station. So under the railway bridge and then the KINGSTON road bridge, a pleasant structure of 1828, widened in 1912 and the twin of that at Richmond. A wooden bridge crossed here at least as long ago as 1318, and the crossing remained up to the 18th century the second Thames bridge from the sea. In 1710 the bridge here was still of wood, for a manuscript of that time states that 'the great Wooden Bridge' had 'in the middle two fair Seates for Passengers to avoid Carts and to sit and enjoy the delightful Prospect.'

A short way above the bridge, lies sunk in the river bed the conduit which brought Cardinal Wolsey's water to Hampton Court from Coombe Wood, $3\frac{1}{2}$ miles from the palace. At least it is presumably still there because between 1803 and 1859 many bargemen complained that their boats grated as they

* At least, Strawberry Hill is generally considered to be the first Gothik Revival building. This, in fact, is not strictly true for the revived style can be traced right back to Wren, Vanbrugh and Hawksmoor. William Kent and others, too, played with the Gothik in a light-hearted, rococo way before Walpole.

passed over it. The conduit contained well over a million pounds weight of lead and was quite a feat of engineering for those days. It indicates the immense luxury of the great palace built by that Ipswich butcher's son to contain rare bathrooms and other sanitary conveniences which kept Hampton Court free from epidemics and thus very popular with the royal inhabitants who followed Wolsey. The water which the conduit carried was said to have medicinal qualities, for a note of 1794 calls it 'efficacious in the gravel, excellent for drinking and washing, but unfit for culinary use' because it turned vegetables black.

Kingston you will no doubt pass by. There is little to see here now except shops, although it is a very old place and was the residence of several Saxon kings. Hence the name. Here Egbert, first king of all England held his Witenagemot in 838 and 'the townischmen' says Leland*, 'have certen knowledge of a few kinges crounid there afore the conqueste', a fact of which the ancient coronation stone in the centre of the town bears witness. At Kingston Sir Thomas Wyat forced a passage in 1558 during his unsuccessful rebellion against Queen Mary and then marched on to London and the scaffold. Here, too, was much fighting in the Civil War, the town being held alternately by the King and by Parliament. Kingston also has the honour of being the last place on record where the ducking stool was used. *The Evening Post* of April 27, 1745, reports: 'Last week, a woman that keeps the King's Head alehouse, Kingston, in Surrey, was ordered by the court to be ducked for scolding, and was accordingly placed in the chair and ducked in the river Thames under Kingston Bridge, in the presence of two or three thousand people.'

Sweeping round the great bend which encloses the Home Park of Hampton Court with its noble trees, we pass on our left the yellow brick waterworks looking like something in a nightmare and then THAMES DITTON, a pleasanter sight with its old church, its hostelry and its island, thick with bungalows and hanging geraniums. The new bridge at HAMPTON COURT

*Leland, who will be interjecting comments all the way up river, was librarian to Henry VIII and has been styled the father of English antiquaries. At the Dissolution of the Monasteries he travelled through the kingdom to search out all monastic records and manuscripts.

comes into view and there on the right the chimneys of the great complex of the Palace serrate the sky. This is the largest palace in England, our own muddled, human, wonderful, beloved Versailles, embodying in rich red brick nearly three centuries of our history. It ceased to be a royal residence in 1760 and, though parts of it are now occupied by distinguished pensioners, much of it has been open to the public since Queen Victoria's time. Let us exercise our privilege and enter.

As we approach through the fine iron gateway with its piers surmounted by the Lion and the Unicorn, we straighten our backs unwittingly and take into ourselves for a moment a sense of regal power and splendour. Ahead lies the oldest part of the Palace:

> With turrets and with towers
> With halls and with bowers.

Everyone knows that the original Palace was built by Wolsey, who, but a few years after it was fully completed in 1520, found it expedient to present it to Henry VIII. Then it contained according to report 'five fair courts' and buildings around them 'so extensive as to admit of two hundred and eighty beds, adorned with rich silk and gold hangings.' The King added the Great Hall among other parts but the general effect as we approach of patterned brickwork, castellations, trellised windows, and arabesqued chimneys must be much the same as it was when the king curvetted up to the entrance arch on his first visit to the Cardinal on his return from the Field of the Cloth of Gold. A Venetian ambassador of the time describes Henry vividly as 'dressed entirely in green velvet, cap, doublet, hose, shoes and everything' As soon as he arrived, the entry goes on, 'he covered his doublet with a handsome gown of green velvet and put on a collar of cut diamonds of immense value; and then dinner was served with incredible pomp. And after this the King put on armour and jousted on a horse covered from head to foot in cloth of gold with a raised pile. In this contest he was victorious, to tremendous applause, especially by the ladies.'

When he started building Wolsey pulled down the manor house which stood here but the bell and cupola were retained from the old building and added to Anne Boleyn's Gateway which leads to the Clock Court. The remarkable clock itself is one of the sights of the place. It was made for Henry VIII in 1540, probably by the French clockmaker, Nicholas Cratzer, It is indeed, more than a clock, being also a calendar beautifully decorated with the signs of the Zodiac, which revolve with the months on the outer dial. It tells you how many days have passed since the start of the year; it shows the phases of the moon and it shows when the moon will be at its height, thus indicating the time of high water at London Bridge, a useful piece of knowledge in the days when the river formed the main line of communication between the Palace and the City. A curiosity of the clock is that the sun is placed to revolve round the earth—a sign of the cosy cosmology of those times.

The Palace became Henry VIII's headquarters. Here a number of his queens endured their sufferings and here his sickly son was born. His daughter Elizabeth was imprisoned here and when she became queen used the Palace a fair amount for pleasure, though it ceased for a time to be the focus of state business. She is known to have celebrated at least two Christmastides at Hampton Court. With James I the court returned to the Palace and in the Great Hall enjoyed the new plays of Shakespeare and Ben Jonson and the stupendous stage sets of Inigo Jones (inspired by his visit to Italy) with their ingenious machines that moved fantastic baroque mountains, woods, cascades and classic pleasure domes. From the Palace Charles I escaped across the river to Southampton and the Isle of Wight. After the Civil War, Charles II, having repaired the Roundhead damages, set up his court here—spectacular and profligate in violent reaction to Puritan austerity.

With William and Mary a great change came to the Palace. Towards the end of the 17th century, Sir Christopher Wren, by this time Surveyor General watching the completion of his new cathedral, was ordered to make considerable additions to the royal residence which had become somewhat dilapidated. He accomplished a fine edifice in spite of limited time, limited means, difficult clients and the problem of fusing his scheme with the old buildings. The east of the Palace was pulled down, including the old Cloister Green Court and the great Tudor gallery, and the new building of splendid brickwork, embellished with quoins and ornaments of Portland stone and pierced with rhythmical sash windows, slowly arose. It was still unfinished at Dutch William's death (he had lost interest when his wife died of small-pox in 1694) and it was completed by Queen Anne and the first two Georges. The two styles—the Tudor and the 'Wrenaissance'—though so different, are strangely coherent. As Sacheverell Sitwell remarks in his *British Architects and Craftsmen:* 'In its two portions . . . we may gather the sensation, respectively, of reading Shakespeare and then discovering the refinements and elegancies of Pope's *Rape of the Lock.*' (It was, incidentally, at the Palace that the young lord of the poetic satire snipped off the beauty's lock).

The Fountain Court is the central feature of Wren's building, one side being a gallery which connects the King's and Queen's apartments. Here Lely's Windsor Beauties hang, portraits of the ladies of Charles II's court, one of whom is unknown and may be Nell Gwynne. The King's staircase has walls and ceilings painted in one vast composition by Antonio Verrio, who also painted the ceilings of the King's bedroom and dressing rooms, of the Queen's drawing room and of the detached banqueting room down by the river. But none of these is so good as the later murals of the Englishman, Sir James Thornhill, decorating the Queen's bedroom and carried out for George I. The finest room in Wren's portion of the palace is undoubtedly the gallery built specially to contain the world-famous tapestry cartoons by Raphael, seven of which have survived and have now settled down, after a restless life, in the Victoria and Albert Museum.

Wren's work was embellished by several great craftsmen of his time and it was surrounded by new gardens. Grinling Gibbons was called from his work at St. Paul's to apply his carving skill; Gabriel Cibber, father of the actor, carried out some sculpture, notably the pediment carving on the particularly fine river elevation and *The Triumph of Hercules over Envy* group which decorates the great triangular pediment on the East front. Cibber also created many stone vases for the gardens. The Frenchman Jean Tijou produced the splendid wrought ironwork of the King's staircase and also the twelve gates now forming a decorative screen down by the river. London and Wise laid out the new gardens in a formal Dutch-cum-Louis-Quatorze way and at the same time the maze was planted, where two centuries later the Three Men enjoyed those adventures which still make the whole world laugh.

Later on in the 18th century the famous Vine was planted and William Kent, that brilliant designer of architectural detail and furniture, carried out some work for George II. The mantelpiece with its Beefeater supports in the Queen's Guard Room is by him and he also remodelled in Gothik taste the George II Gateway. Behind its neo-Gothik façade are two rooms not open to the public, about which Dr. Nikolaus Pevsner has revealed a curious fact*: they contain plaster ceilings designed by Kent in 1732 in *Jacobean* style. Style revivalism of every sort was clearly not confined to the 19th century.

George III did not care for Hampton Court, perhaps because it contained for him too many unhappy associations of his youth when he suffered from the evil-temper of his grandfather, George II, the last monarch to live at Hampton Court. But the depersonalization of the place by the visits of anonymous millions for a century has not yet laid the ghosts of the past. Catherine Howard, distracted with misery, still flies down the Haunted Gallery; Jane Seymour, mother of Edward VI, though she was lucky in having died a natural death, still drifts shimmering white in the light of a taper she carries through the arch of Catherine of Aragon's Door; the infant Edward's nurse, Dame Sibell Penn, whose effigy can be seen in Hampton Church, still turns her spinning wheel in a room of the southwest wing. Those with the gift may also catch at the psychic moment the fleeting sight of Restoration Charles whispering scandalous suggestions into my Lady Castlemain's lovely ear, while his poor Portuguese queen watches with fierce, wounded eyes—or perhaps the second Hanoverian booting his wig across his chamber in an empurpled frenzy.

Back through the far-from-supernatural crowds, past the camera men and the ice-cream tricycles, we note the pleasing, wistaria-covered front of the old *Mitre Hotel* built in the reign of Charles II as a hostel for visitors to the Palace. And so aboard again and under HAMPTON BRIDGE, erected of stone, brick and, concrete shortly before the War to designs by Sir Edwin Lutyens—a competent but uninspired structure, which will improve with weathering. No bridge stood here until the middle

* In *The Architectural Review*, Feb. 1950.

Canaleti's drawing of the 'New Bridge' at Hampton Court, published in 1794

of the 18th century, when the charming rococo affair illustrated in the old print above was built. It seems to have lasted only some 14 years.

The scene ahead is pleasing and typical of the Thames. The gates of MOLESEY LOCK are in sight surrounded and backed by trees, while on the right gardens and more trees come down to the water and to a line of freshly painted cruisers belonging to the members of the Thames Motor Cruising Club. Molesey Lock was first opened in 1815 and, apart from that at Teddington, is the only lock on the river attended by lock-keepers day and night. East Molesey itself is a mere village but contains a cinema, three antique shops and one of the oldest cricket grounds in England. Its name derives from 'the sullen Mole', the tributary which falls into the river just below the bridge.

Having negotiated our first lock we pass on our left an open-air swimming pool followed by a public pleasure garden and set back on our right above the weir lies ASH ISLAND, whose trees embower a small, attractive boat-yard. The island is said to be largely composed of soil dug from the Hampton Waterworks and dumped here when they were built. If you pass through the water dividing this from TAGG'S ISLAND you will come to another weir and just by it you will see a curious fretted building of wood. You will have the immediate desire to lift up its roof to hear what tinkling melody it will play, for it is a genuine Swiss chalet imported in sections from Switzerland and erected here some decades ago, probably at the turn of the century when there was a taste for the exotic, nowhere more playfully expressed than along the river. Upstream a steel bridge, relic of the war years, bars the passage and beyond it you can just make out a public riverside park, one of HAMPTON's most pleasant features.

Back again on the main stream we pass MOLESEY HURST on our left with its Hurst Park racecourse. Its grand-stand and towpath fencing are a disgrace to the river and a bad blot in the landscape, but you can ease the sore by imagining the place as it was in the 18th century. It was a sporting resort even then, though more bucolic, and the meeting place, not of bookies and punters, but of duellers and prize fighters. A letter of the period characterizes those elegant, vigorous, but brutal times:

Breakfasted at Mr. Maule's very early, and went along with him and the Bailie to see the great fight between Belcher and Cribb, at Molesey Hurst, near Hampton. The day was very fine, and we had a charming drive out in our coach-and-four, and beat all the coaches and chaises by the way. We had three hard runs with one post-chaise and four very fine horses, before we could pass it, and drove buggies, horsemen, and all off the road into lanes and doors of houses.

Among those present, the writer continues were:

the Duke of Kent, Mr. Wyndham, Lord Archibald Hamilton (a famous hand, I am told), Lord Kinnaird, Mr. T. Sheridan, etc. etc., and all the fighting men in town, of course . . . the Game Chicken, Woods, Tring, Pitloon, etc. Captain Barclay of Urie received us, and put us across the river in a boat, and he followed with Cribb, whom he backed at all hands. The Hon. Barclay Craven was the judge.

Opposite the racecourse stands GARRICK's VILLA on the far side of the road and below it by the river the small domed temple with classic portico which has been closing the vista ahead of us for some time as we came up-stream. The garden in which it stands is now a small public park but was connected to the rest of Garrick's property by a tunnel under the road. In the temple the great actor once housed the marble statue of Shakespeare executed by Roubiliac in 1758 which is now in the British Museum and for which Garrick himself is said to have posed as a model.

Garrick bought the property here in 1754, consisting of the land and probably a row of timber cottages. These his friends

Robert and James Adam (famed for many fine mansions including Ken Wood and for the Adelphi Terrace below the Strand) used as the basis for the graceful little mansion you now see. The brothers (whom Garrick affectionately addresses in a letter as 'Dear Adelphi') seem to have carried out the alterations here at three different periods and a long time after their third alteration of about 1774—in 1864 to be precise—an addition was made at one side. It has on its main façade a delightful portico standing on an arched podium, all of wood.

Horace Walpole* has talked a lot about this house, of its splendid contents and of the grounds Garrick so lovingly laid out, of the gay but dignified life that went on there, the dinners, the night *fêtes-champêtres* in the illuminated gardens, the gatherings and *conversazione* of the great. 'His house was a rendezvous for excellence of every kind, for Lights of the Church and Guardians of the Law, for the learned, the elegant, the polite and the accomplished in all arts and sciences', writes Tom Davies, the bookseller and publisher, whose life of David Garrick astonished Dr. Johnson by its excellence.

Garrick's life should, indeed, be well worth exploring, for it was a real success story—from the day he plodded up to London at the side of Samuel Johnson 'to try his fate with a tragedy', through his studies for the bar and his failure as a wine merchant until the dramatic night he tried his fortune at Ipswich under the name of Lydall in the part of Aboan in *Oroonoko*. His success was immediate, perhaps because he was unorthodox and 'banished ranting, bombast, and grimace and restored nature, ease, simplicity and genuine humour'. He flourished in his career for thirty spectacular years and then wisely retired, his fame untarnished and his myth established, to his gracious riverside home.

*Horace Walpole should be introduced here for he will be making several comments during our journey. Born 1717, the son of the great Whig, Sir Robert Walpole. Educated at Eton and King's. Adequate private means allowed him to live a dilettante's life. Agreeable, elegant trifler but with considerable literary ability. Wrote a number of books which he printed at his playful, superficially Gothic residence at Strawberry Hill, his most famous work being the romance, *Castle of Otranto*. A great gossip, incurable letter writer and passionate collector of curios. For some years a somewhat cynical and inactive M.P. In 1791 succeeded his nephew to the earldom of Orford. Died at his house in Berkeley Square in 1797.

Beyond Garrick's Ait we come to a grim reach which passes the waterworks, happily shielded in part by PLATTS AIT, whose eastern end is occupied by Thornycroft's boat works. This is just a collection of workshops with no interest, though inside them the industry which goes on must be fascinating to watch. Something of interest, however, stands out in the open between the sheds and set back a hundred yards from the water. It will hold your eye for an instant as you pass, for it is a fine ship's figurehead of a blonde and curly-headed timber god. Passing here one day the author stopped and asked one of the craftsmen why his firm did not make a show of this feature by placing it on the waterfront. He replied: 'We tried that once and you should have seen what happened. Every Monday we found the poor chap in a shocking state with his face rouged and his body dressed up in queer clothes. So we had to move him back out of harm's way'. Perhaps this story will soothe Mr. Epstein for the insults levelled at his statue of Rima in Hyde Park, for it seems that it is not just modern art that rouses the active dislike of our island race but just any poor, mute effigy which cannot answer back.

We soon pass SUNBURY bathing place and a string of wooded islands on our right and so arrive at Sunbury Lock. The river continues below it into a large and attractive basin, full of moored craft and encompassed at its upper end by a wide weir. Sunbury itself looks a sunny little place and is dominated by the 18th-century tower of its church. The nave of the church does not live up to the standard of the tower, for it is a characterless Victorian erection, luckily hidden from the river by an old riverside hotel on whose wide balcony it must be pleasant to laze in the sunshine. Here at Sunbury the Reverend Gilbert White, author of *The Natural History of Selborne* spent several summers.

Above the lock we drift along a narrow cut lined with trees. You will see on the left an old cottage dated 1812, the original lock cottage built when the first lock was opened here by the City of London. An exactly similar one lies at Pentonhook higher up and is still inhabited by the lock-keeper. The elevation of both has great character, partly provided by the monochrome pattern of greys, whites and blacks. Beyond this old cottage the ground was for some years in the early part of the

Old Walton Bridge, designed by White of Weybridge, 1750

19th century a rope walk, where towlines for the river barges were made.

Past many bungalows, some nondescript, some with definite personalities, past a small weir on the right with the pleasant name of Tumbling Bay, we reach WALTON BRIDGE, an ugly iron affair built in 1863 and the least in design of the Thames road bridges, otherwise so markedly good. A rather interesting bridge stood here once, designed by one White of Weybridge. It was completed in 1750 when it was described by a contemporary as follows: 'The happy construction of this bridge was such, that being composed of timbers tangent to a circle of a hundred feet diameter, either of which falling into decay, might, with ease, be unscrewed; and, with equal facility, receive a new substitute, without disturbing the adjoining timbers'. The old engraving above shows the system, which has been applied in a modern timber bridge in the same tradition now standing at Iffley Lock just below Oxford.

WALTON goes back to Saxon days, but contains little of interest today except a Tudor Manor house and, on St. George's Hill near by, the earthworks of a Roman camp. On the left beyond the bridge is an open space, along which is a famous spot known as COWEY (or Causeway) STAKES. Here, according to tradition, Caesar crossed over during his second invasion, after he had battled with Cassivellaunus, the British chieftain. The stakes no longer exist here but one of them lies in the British Museum and is thus described: 'This stake was on 16 October 1777 drawn out of the bottom of the river Thames, in which at least five-sixths of its length was embedded; it stood with several others which (the water being uncommonly low) were then easily to be seen, about one-third of the river's breadth from its south bank, a quarter of a mile above Walton Bridge.'

Caesar left a full account of his battle here in B.C.54. When he arrived at the river, he saw a large force of the British on the opposite bank drawn up to oppose him. 'The bank moreover was planted with sharp stakes, and others of the same kind were fixed in the bend of the river, beneath the water.' This has led many to believe that the two rows of old stakes, first mentioned by the Venerable Bede and still to be seen a hundred years ago, were the originals planted by Caesar's opponents to bar his passage. A Dr. Montagu Sharpe writing in 1906, however, declares that these 'iron-shod posts of Durmast Oak' were either the piers of a bridge built by an early abbot of Westminster or the fence of a swimming way for cattle. It has been recorded that a Speaker of the House of Commons, Arthur Onslow, removed one of these stakes in the late 18th century and had a set of knife and fork handles made from them which, when worked, were as black and heavy as ebony.

Soon the river sweeps round to the right past some very primitive bungalows towards LOWER HALIFORD and SHEP-PERTON, while a cut dug in 1935 and called the DESBOROUGH CHANNEL, runs straight ahead for about half a mile and will take you direct to Shepperton Lock. Above the left bank of this cut lie the grounds of OATLANDS PARK, a place of some historical importance. Henry VIII acquired it by cunning from its youthful owner and developed it in a big way as a palace for Anne of Cleves, largely with materials acquired from the dismantled monasteries. It must have been a stupendous pile rather in the style of Hampton Court and its foundations are said to have spread over fourteen acres. The house has been destroyed by fire several times but has always arisen again. It was the temporary abode at different periods of Edward VI, Elizabeth, James I and Charles I. A succession of noblemen afterwards owned it until it came to the Duke of York in 1790 who rebuilt it as a rococo Gothik fantasy in a Strawberry Hill manner. Here Beau Brummel was a constant visitor. Finally it was turned into an Italianate affair and is now a hotel.

In the magnificent grounds stood, until a few years ago, a curious little structure, one of the few architectural follies along the river and a typical conceit of the 18th century—a garden grotto. It was a remarkable one of its kind and has been fully described and illustrated for posterity by Marcus Whiffen in *The Architectural Review* for May, 1948. Begun about 1780 it took two men six years to build and its great day came when the Duke of York entertained the Emperor of Russia, the King

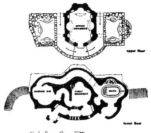

Oatlands Park Grotto

of Prussia and other victors of Waterloo to a supper here under the candelabra which scintillated amidst the decoration of shells, ores and petrifactions.

'Yet it is not as the scene of royal junketings that one mourns the grotto at Oatlands Park', writes Mr. Whiffen:

> The simple fact is that it was a work of art. It was a work of art not merely because its ornaments, the tufa and ammonites and spars and corals and cowries, were applied with a feeling for their distinctive decorative possibilities, but even more because the ingenious involutions of its plan and an extraordinarily skilful use of light gave a sense of mystery and of size to a structure which on paper is not of remarkable dimensions.

The old woodcut reproduced here will give some indication of what it looked like and will perhaps rouse your spleen at the thoughtless and unnecessary vandalism of its demolition.

The DESBOROUGH CHANNEL, though new and artificial, is quite a pleasant passage and will improve in time as the trees grow on its banks. The sweep around by SHEPPERTON however, though it takes longer time to travel, is more interesting. We pass the pretty village group of Halliford and approach Shepperton along by a great slope of grass known as Mrs. Lindsay's Lawn. It belongs to the Manor House and sweeps wide and open right down to the river bank, as all riverside lawns should.

At Shepperton is a landing place where we can tie up if we wish to inspect the village. There are several pubs here, one for the locals and two for more expensive folk. There is also an old church where you may arrive in time to watch with fascination the bellringers at practice in their shirt sleeves. The church was almost completely rebuilt in 1614, though the square tower was

59

added in 1710—not a monument of exceptional interest but it helps to make a pleasing village picture.

Along by a great open field of floodland, through waters at one time much frequented by Isaac Walton and his companions, and we soon link up with the Desborough Channel. The scene below SHEPPERTON LOCK is attractive and gives the effect of a lake—a lake studded with islands, the lowest of which is D'Oyly Carte Island, formerly the property of the producer of the Gilbert and Sullivan operas. Here the Wey Navigation joins the river and here a curious type of ferry crosses the wide water worked manually by a wheel which picks up a chain from the river bed. Here, too, on a spot now covered by the river stood a former church of Shepperton. Dickens's *Dictionary of the Thames* (compiled by the son of the great Charles), alludes to 'a former church standing over the Thames and built on piles (many wills being still extant leaving legacies to add piles to its foundations). *On dit* a flood washed down the former edifice.'

Beyond the lock we pass many bungalows whose setting is improved by a great variety of trees, some of them standing on PHARAOH'S ISLAND (a strange name suggesting that a former owner may have been of gypsy blood). About a mile beyond this island lying on our right is an area called Shepperton Range. This was another favourite place for prize-fighting and *on dit*, as young Dickens would say, that boats would wait by the bank during fights to take the pugilists and their patrons rapidly across the river to the Surrey side if the minions of the law appeared.

CHERTSEY BRIDGE is a dignified structure of Purbeck stone built in the 1780s by James Paine. A bridge has existed here since the 14th century and about 1530 Leland refers to a 'goodly Bridg of Timber newly repairid'. CHERTSEY itself is about a mile away and has little to show. Once upon a time, however, Chertsey held a magnificent Benedictine abbey, of which more will be told in the next chapter. Now only a few stones of it remain, though the abbey tithe-barn survives in a restored condition.

The curfew is still rung at Chertsey every night from Michaelmas to Lady Day on the 14th-century bell, which tolls so many times to denote the day of the month. This old curfew custom is generally believed to have been introduced by William the Conqueror, but it was probably instituted long before his time as a precaution against fire in those remote days when most houses were built of wood and fires were frequent. The curfew itself, or *couvre-feu*, was a metal case placed over the ashes in the hearth to extinguish them. Eight o'clock was the usual time for putting out the fire and going to bed.

Beyond CHERTSEY LOCK for a mile and a half until one reaches the riverside houses of Laleham, the scene is almost rural with the wooded grounds of LALEHAM HOUSE on the right and the open country of the Meads on the left, where the great four-acre Abbey of Chertsey once stood. Laleham House cannot be seen from the river, but, since it is not of great architectural beauty, this is no matter. The house was for centuries the seat of the Earls of Lucan but it is now a convent. About sixty acres of the grounds are now public, leased by the Middlesex County Council to the Staines Council. Notice the simple metal railings painted white, which divide the road from the grass area running to the river—a good, rare piece of municipal furnishing; they form a decorative linear element in the landscape set, as they are, against the dark background of trees.

A ferry crosses at LALEHAM, the position being marked on the left by a delightful Georgian ferry cottage with old handmade tiles on its roof of that satisfying colour and texture which modern building materials so rarely achieve. If we land by the towpath on the right, a short stroll will bring us into Laleham village—some houses and cottages of charm, a shop or two and a brick church, Norman in origin but having a square brick tower of the 18th century, rather crudely restored in 1932, and also an interesting Tudor chapel of the Lucan family. In the churchyard are some old gravestones worth an inspection, in particular one of the 18th century carved with cherubim, near the south porch. Here, too, is the family grave of Matthew Arnold, poet of the upper river who was born here in 1822, the son of Dr. Arnold of Rugby, who founded our public school system.

The banks from Laleham to Staines are much built up with Edwardian houses and modern bungalows. On the way we negotiate PENTONHOOK LOCK, the highest upstream of the Old City Locks and another pleasant stage in the journey. Here the original course of the river turns in a strange hook containing an unspoiled and wooded island and the decorative weirs of the Thames Conservancy with the intriguing, rhythmical forms of their sluice machinery. This is a charming spot with its 1814 cottage and well-kept gardens.

Between here and Staines stands a relic of the days when the towpath was used for towing—a structure of timbers below which a boat could lie safely protected from the towlines passing over it.

Modern STAINES is a crowded, ugly town which has made little of its riverside situation. The most disharmonious blot is the modern cinema which stands with its back right up against the river just below the bridge. If you step ashore here and follow the line of the bridge into Middlesex, bearing left, you will soon come to the best part of the town—a pleasing road of old houses with a villagey character which will bring you to the Gothic Revival church of 1828. This is not particularly striking, though it is interesting in having a tower which stands on the base of a structure built in 1631, supposedly by Inigo Jones, who lived at Staines for a time.

STAINES BRIDGE itself is a good monumental work of granite opened in 1834 by William IV. It was executed by the son of John Rennie, one of the great early engineers, famous for his London, Waterloo and Southwark bridges and the Kennet and Avon Canal, among many other works.

Many bridges have existed here right back to Roman times. Staines was then called *Ad Pontes* which suggests that there were two bridges here, one of which must have carried the Roman road from London to Silchester and Bath. The name Staines, from the Saxon word *Stana*, a stone, may have derived from the stone base on which the original Roman timber bridges were built, or perhaps from the paving of the Roman highway, or, more likely, from the historic London Stone which stands on the Middlesex bank a short way above the bridge.

3
Looking Back

BEYOND STAINES BRIDGE, like some bored but brutal potentate, a monstrous gas-holder subdues the gentle river—a fortunately rare break-through of industry. Opposite on the right is another symptom of our cultural decadence—a dull municipal garden, which gracelessly ignores the river's proffered gift of charm. Nevertheless, an object of great interest stands there by the paddling pool. This is the LONDON STONE marking the former upper limit of the City of London's jurisdiction over the Thames on the border of Middlesex and Buckinghamshire. At one time the stone bore the date 1285, for no known reason, since the care of the lower river had been vested in the Corporation of the City by Richard I in 1197—a care the City guarded jealously for seven centuries. The stone is still inscribed 'God preserve ye City of London', but it is itself not medieval, dating apparently from the 17th century.

Then about a mile upstream beyond BELL WEIR LOCK lies the famous field of RUNNYMEDE. Here, as everyone knows, the Magna Charta was signed (or rather sealed, because King John could not write) and a significant clause in that charta to us just now states that the great rivers of the kingdom were to be free to all men.

We are at a part of the journey which is historically of the first importance. Therefore let us moor for an hour or so beyond the modern obtrusions of Staines at the upper end of Runnymede. Just lie on your back in the sun and dream your own fantasies of the old days or read, if you wish, this true story of the Thames—both as an epitome of the whole of English history and as a revelation of how men have attempted through the centuries to control these inexhaustible waters. Such an outline will provide a string on which to thread our necklace of

63

impressions. Much of the information has been culled from
Hilaire Belloc's classic of Thames literature, *The Historic Thames*,
and from Fred Thacker's *Thames Highway*, a standard work of
1914 on the river's conservancy.

Why has the Thames been so important in our history?
Belloc gives the answer:

Partly because it was the main highway of Southern England, partly because it
looked eastward towards the Continent from which the national life has been
drawn, partly because it was better served by the tide than any other channel,
but mainly because it was the chief among a great number of closely connected
river basins, the Thames Valley has in the past supported the government and the
wealth of England.

From the beginning of human activity in this island the whole length of the
river has been set with human settlements never far removed one from the other;
for the Thames ran through the heart of South England, and wherever its banks
were secure from recurrent floods it furnished those who settled on them with
three main things which every early village requires: good water, defence, and
communication. The importance of the first lessens as men learn to dig wells and
to canalize springs; the last two, defence and communication, remain attached to
river settlements to a much later date, and are apparent in all the history of the
Thames.

It is mainly as a means of communication, as a continuous,
united and uniting highway, that the river has been important,
especially since Christianity came. Of that, the curious shapes
on the maps of many riverside parishes give evidence, for they
come down to the river as long strips—tongues that stretch
from the hinterland to lick the water. A typical case is that of
the parish of Fawley in Buckinghamshire, which achieves
narrow access for wharfage to the river opposite Remenham
Church, just below Henley.

As a highway the Thames possessed a special advantage compared with other rivers. Every navigable river divides naturally
into three parts. The lower part is separated from the upper two
by the first bridge—the point at which a town will grow. On
the Thames this point, of course, is London Bridge. The second
is the navigable but non-tidal part above the first bridge and
that is where the Thames had its advantage, because, in proportion to its total length, this part is greater than that of any
other of Europe's shorter rivers. Moreover, it is fairly easily

64

navigable both up and down stream, because its average fall is only 17 inches in the mile.

Until the Thames and Severn Canal was dug in the late 18th century and absorbed much of the water of the upper stream, it was indeed possible to navigate commercial craft right up to Cricklade. From Cricklade you could journey in a long day across country to the navigable part of the Severn. Thus there was an easy route from east to west through the wealthiest, most fertile and most populated area of the island.

The third part of a river is contained in the head waters where the stream is too shallow for navigation. In the case of the Thames this unusable part is very short—no more than some fifteen miles.

The people of the Middle Ages used the river as a road more than those of any other period. Then it must have been a bustling, lively highway when wool, hides and stone from the Cotswolds, cheese and meat from the valley farms and the craftsmen's produce from the great religious houses were carried down river, while much more slowly and laboriously came upstream from London such wares as Cheapside cloth, silks from France, wines, spices and other luxuries for the abbeys.

As a military obstacle the Thames is again different from other rivers of its kind. In most rivers, the two sections—the upper, where crossings are easy and frequent and the lower, where fords become rare—merge gradually into one another. In the Thames the two sections are sharply articulated at Oxford, above which the river is by no means easy to cross, in spite of its shallowness and narrowness. This is due to the marshy, insecure nature of the soil on either bank. As Belloc points out:

The loneliness of the stretch below Kelmscott is due to the original difficulty of this kind and the one considerable settlement upon the upper river at Lechlade stands upon the only place where firm ground approaches the bank of the river ... Perhaps the highest point at which it had to be crossed at one chosen spot is to be discovered in the word Somer*ford* Keynes, but the ease with which the water itself could be traversed is apparent rather in the absence than in the presence of names of this sort upon the upper Thames.

The only other ford names above Oxford are Swinford Shifford and Duxford and Shifford may equally well have applied to the Great Brook as to the river.

Below Oxford the river was originally passable only at certain points before the bridges came—at Sandford, Abingdon (the part by the bridge has been called Burford), Appleford, a long gap until Shillingford and then Wallingford. There were other fords below this (Cookham, for example, has provided relics which prove that it was a very ancient one) and even the tidal parts could be forded at certain times and at certain points. Wallingford, however, was all-important as a crossing because it was the lowest point which was always dependable. It is therefore a key point in Thames history—a node of military strategy and commerce. Thus Wallingford produced two major events in British history—the crossing of the Thames by the Conqueror and the successful struggle of Henry II against Stephen. Before then it had been used by the Saxon kings. Only when the bridge was built at Abingdon did the importance of Wallingford decline.

In its use as a defensive barrier, the river shows only two fortifications directly dependent on the river. The first is Dorchester with its Sinodun earthworks, a primeval one, and the second Windsor.

Windsor Castle was built by the Conqueror, though the artificial mound on which the Round Tower stands may be prehistoric. William completed the job at speed, for it was finished within four years after Hastings and before the Saxons had been fully subjugated. He chose this spot because it was just the right distance from London—the purpose of the castle being to act as a warden of the capital. Moreover, here was a firm mound of chalk surrounded by uncertain clay; it was accessible by road and water, and, to help defence, on one side lay the river and on the other uninhabited wastelands (later to become the Forest, useful for hunting as well as defence). The Castle was of great value to William and later also to John in his struggle with the Barons, when he held this point as a projection right down into enemy territory.

Of the other military establishments of the Thames not deliberately formed to depend on the river, Oxford and Wallingford were the most important. Oxford was a strategic centre from early times, for the Saxons, the Danes and the Normans all fought here. We have already mentioned Wallingford.

Reading was a special case in having been mainly a civil and monastic settlement without great strategic value, and, although it did have the military advantage of standing in the peninsula between two joining rivers—the Thames and the Kennet—it never seems to have been seriously held as a base.

Consider now the economic development of the river. Right back as far as we can see settlements have existed along the river, but the time of the greatest settlements, the time of the river's glory, was the medieval days—the days of the great monasteries.

Three Benedictine monasteries were built on the Thames during the 7th century—at Westminster, Chertsey and Abingdon. These were the founders of civilization along the valley. Westminster and Abingdon were sacked during the Danish invasions. Chertsey was utterly destroyed and its ninety monks massacred. But about 950 Chertsey arose from its ruins and was re-colonised from Abingdon. Then the Conquest came to give them a new vitality. Except for their early troubles, they flourished for nearly a thousand years, when they fell at last and for ever under the destructive hand of our greatest royal bully, Bluff King Hal.

Other establishments followed these three as results of their pioneering work—the great post-Conquest houses of Reading, Dorchester, Osney, Rewley and Eynsham and a string of smaller, dependent foundations—the friaries, nunneries, priories, schools, hospitals and cells, many of whose remains we shall pass on our upstream voyage.

But Henry wanted independence, power and money; his followers were greedy for land; public opinion was weak and the Church, uncertain of itself under the new nationalism and too often neglectful of its sacred duties, was old and small in numbers (there were but some 8,000 members in a population of 4 million). The result was the most brief and drastic social and economic upheaval in our history. It all occurred within a few years and it was an enormity. Of all the river foundations in this period of looting and destruction, Westminster alone survived. Of the others only a few scattered stones now suggest their former size and splendour.

In the end it was not the King but the oligarchy of squires which acquired land, wealth and power and finally ruled

England. Eventually their greatest champion was Oliver ap Williams *alias* Cromwell who had curiously close connections with the Thames, and not only because it was along the river line that he fought his first battles, or because it was in Windsor Park that he trained his Model Army.

At the beginning of the 16th century a Morgan Williams was keeping a pub by the riverside at Putney. Here also lived a certain Crumwell, a smith. It seems that Crumwell's son, Thomas, fell in love with Morgan's sister and that Morgan himself set up house with Katherine, Crumwell's daughter. Thomas went off on an adventure to Italy, took up money-lending and, being a clever rogue, came to the notice of Wolsey, thus giving us another river association with the family in that Thomas must have attended court at Hampton. His ruthlessness and perhaps his faithfulness to his master, recommended him to Henry VIII, for after Wolsey's fall the King used Thomas as his chief lieutenant in suppressing the monasteries. This gave Thomas the chance to embezzle on a large scale.

At the height of his power Thomas Crumwell raised from his Putney obscurity his nephew Richard Williams, son of his sister Katherine, whom he set up as a landed gentleman at Huntingdon in 1538. Thomas, now Earl of Essex, fell from favour and was executed. Five months later his nephew managed to revive the barony and was soon firmly established as one of the country's richest men. His son Henry maintained the fortune and became Queen Elizabeth's sycophant. In 1603 he died, leaving the fortune to his two sons Robert and Oliver, who had now managed to rid themselves of the patronym of Williams and had established themselves in their time and in all the history books of the future by the more distinguished-sounding name of Cromwell.

After the days of the landed plutocracy with their wavering fortunes, came in the 18th century another great social change brought, now, by coal and iron—the Industrial Revolution. The landowners were superseded, or absorbed by, the rising class of manufacturers and credit monopolists. The canals inaugurated this new age by providing a reliable and cheap means of transport, and the Thames, by its links with the new waterway system, enjoyed a brief revival as a communication—brief because in less than three generations the railways had beaten the canals and brought them at last to the charming but wasteful state of dereliction in which we find them today. This usurpation by the railways, as we have already noted, did at least help to preserve many old beauties of the river.

The railways, nevertheless, greatly affected some of the Thames towns. Whereas throughout their history the riverside settlements had been fairly evenly spaced and populated, in the 19th century many dwindled in importance while others expanded to elephantine size. Though Oxford and Reading did obtain a certain lead through the development of the waterways, the main developments of these towns, as of others throughout the country, were brought by the 'Railers.'

Wallingford, at one time the largest settlement of the upper river, has dwindled to a small market town, whereas Reading, once comparatively insignificant, is now the largest and most industrialised of the urban centres along the river, Oxford coming a close second. Near London, the river towns expand as metropolitan dormitories. Whereas in 1801 Henley housed 2,000 souls, Maidenhead contained half that number. Today Henley has 6,600 and Maidenhead 17,500. The relative growths of Reading and Abingdon are significant: at one time twin monasteries (Abingdon being by far the larger), then twin corporations, in the beginning of the 19th century their ratio of population was three to one. The railway discovered Reading but not Abingdon. Today the ratio is fourteen to one.

We are back at the Staines gas-holder as a symbol of the new order. But expanded Reading shows the worst break-through into the pleasant river landscape, which has otherwise been on the whole so miraculously preserved. How we can continue to preserve it is discussed later on during a second pause on our way.

* * *

Meanwhile let us look at the past of the river from a special aspect—that of the human control of, and conflicts about, the water itself.

We who voyage on the river in peace and security and pass through those well-regulated locks with a smile and a nod from the lock-keeper and no more discomfort than a few wetted fingers, may not always realise how tough, dangerous and quarrelsome was the former river life ever since the early settlements

Old Hart's Weir, now no more

were formed, nor how recent is the organized river control.

The pound-lock—by which you can raise or lower craft from one level to another by means of a kind of cistern capable of being filled or emptied and entered through gates at either end —was apparently just one more invention of that extraordinary genius Leonardo da Vinci, which he applied in the Mortesana Canal built to supply Milan with water round about the year 1488. It was not used in England until 1563 in the Exeter Canal, and even then was not applied on a large scale until the Canal Era opened in the second half of the 18th century. On the Thames, the first pound-locks were erected in the middle of the 17th century during the reign of James I between Burcot and Oxford.

Before that, so-called locks had been used on the river for centuries, but they were not locks in our sense of the word but merely rough staunches or weirs lying across the stream, made of closely spaced timber stakes filled with chalk and stones. These stemmed back the water at certain points, sometimes to intercept fish, sometimes to create a head of water for milling and sometimes to create a floating depth for navigation.

Long and bitter have been the contentions over these weirs through the years between fishermen, millers and boaters. And bitter, too, have been the perpetual complaints of the riverside people over the continual heightening of the weirs, bringing floods to drive them from their homes and to ruin their crops.

These weirs originally did little to control the flow of water

Weir paddles

but when barge traffic grew, openings were formed in the stakes some ten or twenty feet wide into which movable tackle was fixed. These were called flash locks on account of the flash or flush of water that could be let through the openings when a passage for a boat was required, or when flood water needed release. When the paddles and rymers were pulled up a great rush of water poured through. When this had subsided to some degree, a boat going upstream would be hauled up by a rope attached either to a gang of men, to a horse, or to a windlass. Going down the boat merely shot the rapid. The trouble with this system was that the waste of water was enormous because almost the whole height of water along the upper reach, acting like a phenomenally long pound-lock stretching for several miles up to the next weir, was poured away. In dry times, days and sometimes weeks were needed to replenish the reach after each flush, and so both milling and navigation were seriously impeded.

The waste of water through this primitive form of control led to serious rivalry between the millers and bargemen, mainly because both required dams in the same places—that is wherever sharp falls in the river bed created fast streams. The millers were gradually allowed to levy tolls on passing barges to compensate them for the loss of water power. The boats needed flashes to float them over distant shallows which the millers grudgingly spared for a fee, but even then a wretched navigator might be robbed of the flash for which he had paid by another miller further down stream.

Right up to and well into the 19th century millers were insisting on their control of the flow of water. This is revealed in an official enquiry of 1865 when a bargeowner complains that 'the millers stand and laugh at our men when they cannot go on, after they have paid for getting the water. We had a case last summer where it cost 18s. (I think there were six boats to share it) to get water; and at Sandford Lock the miller's man stood and laughed at our man and said: "Thank you for bringing the water", and he had to lie there till the next flash'.

Through recorded history attempts have been made by authority to bring some sort of control of the river and to resolve such conflicts. Only in our own century has the last attempt of all been fully successful—and then at a time when the river is no longer a great highway and only a few mills stand and grind.

All down the years we hear lamentations and complaints about the abuse of the river. In 1580 one John Bishop made a spirited attack on the vested interests of the river and presented it in high places. It is specially interesting in being the oldest known personal survey of the river. It seems to have had no effect for in 1585 Bishop renewed his complaints, this time direct to Queen Elizabeth. He did so in an unusual way, for he tried to bring home the seriousness of the situation, especially the dangers of navigation, in the emotive form of verse. Here are two typical excerpts from his forty-three quatrains:

	One ffarmer hath a Lock in store
A Locke of great	That hath made many a Child to weepe
Murther (Marlow)	Ther mothers begg from dore to dore
	Their ffathers drowned in the deepe
	Then being drowned they bury them there
Swine and dogges do	where doggs and swyne then do them finde
eat mens fleshe	their fleshe they eat and all to teare
	which is contrarie to mankinde

Even this heartcry met with little reaction, for half a century later comes another tirade in the verse of John Taylor, known as the Water Poet, for he was a waterman. In his book *Thame Isis* published in 1632, he shows us that socialism is a very old, conservative conception, for he writes:

And for the good to England it hath done,
Shall it to spoyle and ruine be let runne?
Shall private persons for their gainfull use,
Ingrosse the water and the land abuse?

During the 17th century the river between Oxford and Burcot (just below Clifton Hampden) became quite impassable and
at last some limited legislation was passed. In 1605 the Oxford-
Burcot Commission was inaugurated, being strengthened in
1623. Though its activities were confined to a fairly short length
of river, it is distinguished for having built the first pound-locks
on the Thames and also for having instituted a continuous
towpath through its district to be 'without hindrance, trouble
or impeachment of any person' in that boats 'must of necessity
in some places and at some times be hauled up by the strength of
men, horses, winches and other engines.' The pound-locks it
built were at Iffley, Sandford and Swift Ditch (the old Abingdon by-pass, now disused).

For a hundred and fifty years nothing much happened. Then
things boiled up again owing to the exactions of the weir owners
and the ruffianism of the boaters, whose successive gangs of
hauliers working the towpath (known as Scufflehunters) were
the terror of the riverside communities. In 1751 was formed
the first permanent general Authority, an unwieldy body which
became known twenty years later as the Thames Commissioners, ancestors of the present Thames Conservancy. This
body was at first ineffectual, having no power to build pound-
locks. Freight rates rose to unbearable heights and so in 1770
the Commissioners obtained new powers to make and acquire
towpaths and to build new pound-locks, at least above the
London Stone. Their earliest work was the present series of
locks between Boulter's and Sonning, excluding that at Cookham, which came much later.

In 1774 the first special houses for lock-keepers were built,
mere wooden huts overlooking the new locks, which were crude
affairs with sides of sloping turf (You can still see the type on the
Kennet and Avon Navigation). These locks were poorly constructed of deal, unlike their sturdy Jacobean forebears of oak
built by the Oxford-Burcot Commission, and were already in
decay after nine years of use. In 1780 a proper towpath was

73

established as far as Pangbourne and in this year, too, the first project was submitted for towing barges by steam power—a sign of the Industrial Revolution which had already begun to change the face of the country. In 1795 another Act was passed to create new locks and a proper, continuous, public horse-tow-path, as well as to regularize tolls.

With the building of the canals and with the limited improvements of the Thames Commissioners, the river enjoyed a brief spell of fifty years of fair commercial activity. Then the railways arrived and the decline began. In 1853 the lock-keepers' wages were reduced by half, though they were allowed to retain the tolls from pleasure traffic for their own use—a significant pointer this to the growing use of the Thames for pleasure boating, a use which the rival railways had made possible in that they brought the river within reach of the whole population.

Conditions were soon bordering on ruin and it is reported that in 1862 only nine vessels had passed from the Thames and Severn Canal into the river up to the month of May. Obviously something had to be done.

In 1866 the whole navigable river from Cricklade down to Yantlet Creek was placed under the authority of the Conservancy Board. The preamble to the Act complained that the Thames Commissioners were too numerous and did not form a body corporate, that all river works were in a bad and dangerous state, that their income was not sufficient even to cover expenses and that the time had come to place the whole river under one management. New revenue was to be raised from each of the five Metropolitan Water Companies, no letting of sewage into the river was to be allowed, many locks were to be rebuilt and tolls regularized.

In 1885 came the Thames Preservation Act, which is significant in showing that by now the river, though it had lost most of its commercial traffic, had become firmly established as a holiday resort. It is the first Act specifically directed towards 'the preservation of the River above Teddington lock for purposes of public recreation and for regularizing the pleasure traffic therein.' The official enquiry which preceded this Act makes fascinating reading. It reveals that though the old conflicts between millers and boaters were over, new conflicts were

74

rising between the public and the owners of riparian property. Here is an entertaining extract, a genuine period piece, from the minutes of the Select Committee which sat in 1884:

Sir Gilbert Augustus Clayton East, Bart: I do not object to the public using the river, because that I have no right and no wish to do, and I rather like to see them enjoying themselves. From 1858 to 1862 I was at Eton, and during that time the public practically did not exist; the only boats then seen were Eton boys' and masters', soldiers', and a few residents' . . . I think it was somewhere about 1866 that the Guards Club was started; and that first brought people down to Maidenhead in any numbers . . . In 1878 the river had become so unpleasant, not from the number of public, though that had something to do with it, but from the way they treated you, that I gave up making these trips at all. They began to be most abusive and disagreeable . . . My complaint is not of the public coming to use the river, but of the class who come. It is so totally different. You used never to have any unpleasant remarks.

Chairman: What proportion of the public do you complain of in this way?

Sir Gilbert: That is what I have often wanted to know; whether these people were naturally savages; or whether they become savage when they come on the river.

Chairman: What proportion of the public who use the Thames in this way possess this qualification of savages of which you speak?

Sir Gilbert: I distinctly say it is not the working class; because if you ever see any of the working class on the river, which you do on Bank holidays, they are always very well behaved. I cannot tell what class it is. I believe it is a class of savages born on purpose.

Chairman: Is the proportion one in ten, or one in five, or what proportion are the people who make the river a nuisance?

Sir Gilbert: I should say that many of the respectable people are giving up using the river; it is getting more every year that these savages use the river. It is difficult to speak of any proportion. I will speak of what I myself know at Hurley. What brought them there was the opening of the Marlow Railway in 1878. They did not find that out for a few years; but after a while they did.

Chairman: When you say you delight in seeing the public happy on the river, you at the same time tell us that the river is no longer endurable because of the public?

Sir Gilbert: Not of the public, but of a certain class of the public . . . There are apparently two classes of roughs which frequent the river; one class clearly belongs to the London ' 'Arry', by the absence of the letter H; the other is a superior class if you can judge by their clothing and their manner, and yet these are the people who do as much, if not more, damage, than the others. The real river roughs offend by their appearance, their language, and their deeds.

Chairman: Which do you call the real river rough, the first or the second class?

Sir Gilbert: The real river roughs are the first class. They now dress in short trousers not reaching down so far as their knees, and a jersey without sleeves. When, as often happens, there is a difficulty in keeping the apology for trousers in their place, they appear almost absolutely naked, and yet these savages are often accompanied by women; their language is as disgusting as their appearance.

Chairman: I want to know the rate of the disorderly persons to the orderly persons who use the river.

Sir Gilbert: I do not know the river at Maidenhead on Sunday, because I do not go there, but from my knowledge of the river I should say that on a Sunday the majority are these objectionable people. I am not speaking of a week-day. On a week-day I should say the majority are respectable people. One Sunday I was down at my Reach, and three lockfuls of boats came through one after another. A steam launch came through. I suppose they are not all as well behaved as they should be. There was a table fitted up in front, with two men and two women, and they went up sitting at this table with a bottle of Champagne; in another hour they came back. They had consumed two bottles of Champagne; and they were then followed through the lock by another launch which had a cabin to it In this cabin was a middle aged man lying down fast asleep with an empty Champagne bottle by his side. I have not so much complaint to make of these steam-launches, because they do not offend very much; they pass by and are gone, but the rowing boats hang about. They come up from Marlow, and hang about all day.

Not surprisingly, the Committee found the attitude of such riparian property owners a trifle biased and hardly in accord with the spirit of Magna Charta.

In 1887 the Conservancy decline a request to display advertisements at the locks, thus setting a precedent for which we must be grateful. In 1894 comes a long and complicated Act to tie up and perpetuate all the former enactments since 1770 and to add new legislation. In 1898, the first prizes are offered for attractive lock gardens. An Act of 1908 finally brings us up-to-date, for by this the Thames eastward of a point about three hundred and fifty yards below Teddington Lock was transferred to the control of the Port of London Authority. The Thames Conservancy was at the same time reconstituted to look after the whole of the 135 miles of river and the watershed above Teddington.

And so on our way again, made smooth at last by the paternal vigilance of the modern conservators.

4

Staines to Maidenhead

AN EARLY SUMMER MORNING in the year 1215. In the wide field below COOPER'S HILL the rebel lords have set up their camp among the buttercups after their march from London along the old Roman military road. It is a grand sight. The rows of round tents in bright and variegated colours with pennants atop stand out dramatically against the fresh green background of the wooded hill. Blue smoke from the cooking fires rises straight up to mingle with the banks of early morning mist, portending a day of heat. There is a good deal of noise—much shouting and jesting, the occasional clank of armour, the neighing and stamping of the sturdy shires and the rhythmical ring of a blacksmith's hammer. Suddenly the stir increases. The King! The King! Along the track from Windsor in brilliant panoply the royal *cortège* comes jogging. The hubbub dies down and the men stand silent now and gaze up curiously at the fixed and angry face of the third Plantagenet.

Of course, this is all dreaming. But it is possible that the king that morning did indeed pass over the very spot on which we are now standing to read the inscription on one of the pair of stone piers set up here over seven hundred years later. The finely chiselled Roman lettering states: 'In these Meads on 15th June 1215, King John at the instance of deputies from the whole community of the realm, granted the Great Charter, the earliest of constitutional documents, whereunder ancient and cherished customs were confirmed and abuses redressed, the administration of justice facilitated, new provisions formulated for the peace, and every individual perpetually secured in the free enjoyment of his life and property.'

Probably the astute king did not risk so close a contact with the enemy but camped on the opposite side of the river at ANKERWIKE. Tradition says that the Barons presented the great document of freedom to the King, not at RUNNYMEDE itself but on MAGNA CARTA ISLAND, where a grey Gothic Revival cottage now stands. The cottage, it is said, contains a large rough stone on which the Charter is supposed to have been sealed. The stone is inscribed: 'Be it remembered that on this island, in June, 1215, King John of England signed Magna Charta; and in the year 1834, this building was erected in commemoration of that great event by George Simon Harcourt, Esq., Lord of the Manor, and then High Sheriff of the County.'

It is good to know that this historic open space of Run Mede, the Council Meadow, can now never be built upon or spoiled. In 1929 it was presented to the Nation and placed under the administration of the National Trust as a public place. At each end of the meadow pairs of small, well-built lodges of brick and stone in a kind of Georgian style have been built, between which stand the lettered stone piers. The designer was the late Sir Edwin Lutyens, famous for his country houses of a departed era. We shall discover other examples of his work further up river.

Just beyond Runnymede on the left we pass the boundary between Surrey and Berkshire, along whose border we shall now wind for a hundred miles. We shall find that Berkshire is essentially a county of brick, especially of brick applied to domestic architecture, whose excellent tradition has flourished here since the 16th century when the cloth trade prospered in the county. It is also a county rich in ancient almshouses, a number of which we shall be visiting.

Just beyond the border stands the *Bells of Ouzeley*—a very old inn associated with the highwayman who once haunted this district. On the right the bungalows begin again, stretching for two miles right up the weir stream and round the Ham Fields. Before entering Old Windsor Lock let us step onto the towpath on the left and plunge down a narrow path between hedges. Soon we shall come to the church of OLD WINDSOR END whose spire has been visible from the river. The church is of no great merit in itself and was restored by the Victorian architect Sir Gilbert Scott with his customary ruthlessness. The

Above Staines is the historic open space of Runnymede where Magna
Carta was signed in 1215. The field is now preserved as a public open space
by the National Trust. Here you can relax in the sunshine as completely as
this lad who has cycled from some airless room in the metropolis to dream,
perhaps, about the past of these inexhaustible waters.

FACING PAGE, TOP LEFT, the reach at Datchet where the Home
Park comes to the water. TOP RIGHT, a misty morning below Romney Lock; Eton College Chapel lies in the distance. BELOW LEFT,
the cast iron bridge of 1824 at Windsor and the Castle rising behind.
THIS PAGE, TOP LEFT, Romney Lock with its ranges of granite steps.
TOP RIGHT, the bosky lock of Boveney. ABOVE LEFT, the footbridge
over the weir at Romney Lock; the Round Tower of Windsor Castle
is in the distance. ABOVE RIGHT, Eton Wet Bobs in Cookham Lock.

ABOVE, the Victorian fantasy of Oakley Court below Bray. LEFT, Monkey Island with its 18th-century pavilion built for the third Duke of Marlborough and now part of a private house. FACING PAGE, the simple handrail with its decorative curls at Bray Lock weir is a typical example of good Thames trim.

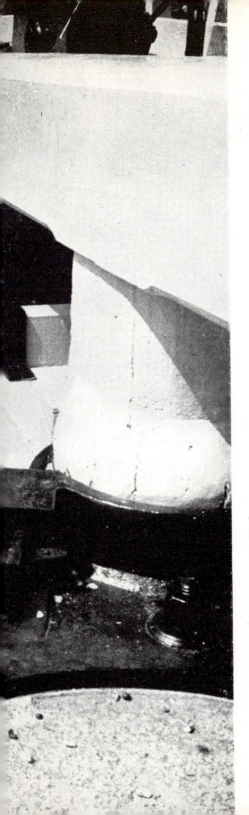

The upper gates of Bray Lock. Robust iron and timber forms with a tough, practical job to do, they are at the same time satisfying to look at and add to the visual pleasures of the river. Being in that nautical tradition of design from boats to bollards, from sea-walls to lighthouses, they create beauty without intention.

85

ABOVE, the reach at Bray; the village with its old church and almshouses, strange neighbours to centres of cosmopolitan luxury, lies behind the trees. BELOW, a vintage house-boat of the river, built in the heyday of the middle class, still floats under the trees near Romney Lock.

churchyard, however, has a sweet, remote and melancholy air. Here we shall find the simple tomb of the lovely Perdita, immortalised by Reynolds, Gainsborough and Romney and once renowned for her part in *The Winter's Tale*. The Fair Shepherdess they called her, but her more mundane name was plain Mrs. Mary Robinson.

She wrote her memoirs, which were first published in 1801; from these it is clear that her evident self-pity was justified because she seems to have had a very hard time. Being badly treated by her husband, she gave in at last to the oglings of the Prince Regent ('Your fat fwend' as Beau Brummel called him so unceremoniously) and became his mistress. But he soon tired of her and left her in a solitude at first alleviated by £500 a year. At 26 she took a serious rheumatic disease from which she suffered for the rest of her life, and died painfully at an early age. But she gave something to the world in her short life—not merely her personal beauty and her acting ability, but much poetry too. Under the name of Sappho, Mary Robinson wrote a poem each day for some time in *The Morning Post* and one year she even attained the honour of having a piece included in Southey's *Annual Anthology*. Coleridge was very impressed with her work but then he was in love with her. It is not great stuff but it has the charm of the period and has earned a small but permanent place in the archives of the Romantic Movement.

A Victorian writer describes meeting an old labourer in this churchyard, 'who had wheeled a barrow, heavily laden with autumn prunings up the broad gravel walk close to where we sate.' He tells the writer:

There's not much in the churchyard to please you; only, maybe, like the rest of the gentry, you want to see what we used to call the tomb of the Fair Shepherdess . . . She was a play-actor once . . . They say a king's love fell upon her like a mildew, and, for all her beauty, withered her up; and then; and then she died, poor thing—bad enough off too . . . I can tell over the inscription to you—'Mrs. Mary Robinson, author of poems, and other literary works; died on the 26th of December, 1800, at Englefield Cottage, in Surrey, aged 43 years.' . . . Why, you'll hardly believe it, *now*, when the gentry come and ask which is 'Perdita's' tomb, and I tell 'em, maybe they'll hardly damp their shoes to look at it, and ask each other what poems 'twas she wrote, and no one knows—not one can tell! But some fifty years ago, I've seen some, and from the Castle, too, who would tell them all over plain enough.

Poor Sappho! poor Perdita! poor Shepherdess! You shall at least be remembered here by a few of the bitter lines you wrote for your own memorial:

Oh Thou! whose cold and senseless heart
Ne'er knew affection's struggling sigh,
Pass on, nor vaunt the Stoic's art,
Nor mock this grave with tearless eye.

No wealth had she, no power to sway;
Yet rich in worth, and learning's store:
She *wept her summer hours away,*
She heard the wintry storm no more.

OLD WINDSOR has nothing more to show, but it has an ancient history. Long ago it contained a palace of the Saxon kings where Edward the Confessor once kept his court. On again now and through OLD WINDSOR LOCK and down the charming New Cut as picturesque as an old canal. Then we reach Albert Bridge and beyond that pass a formal line of trees skirting the Home Park of Windsor on the Berkshire side. Through the trees we can now see the great grey mound of Windsor Castle. On the right we pass DATCHET with its pleasant public green by the riverside backed by Georgian houses and known as The Beach. Under Victoria Bridge, wondering if it was just about here whither Falstaff was carried in a basket to be thrown into the Thames and 'cooled, hissing hot, in that surge, like a horseshoe.'

Under one of the ugly railway bridges of the river and there round a bend ROMNEY LOCK lies snugly. On the right is a prospect across the Eton playing fields of the College Chapel, while straight ahead, at the end of the cut beyond the lock, the bold squat cylinder of the Round Tower of the Castle rears up —not, incidentally, quite as round as it looks.

Of WINDSOR CASTLE, as of Hampton Court, one could write a book for it must be richer in royal and historical associations than almost any other building in the country. Building, one says, but it is in fact a whole jumble of buildings, not all, by any means, so very old. In fact the pile as seen from across the river gives little impression of its earlier appearance, for it is largely the work of Sir Jeffrey Wyatville, carried out between 1824 and 1840, that is from the end of the reign of George IV,

Ancient Windsor Castle

through that of William IV up to the beginning of that of Victoria.

Wyatville (1766-1840) was the nephew of James Wyatt (1746-1813), a more famous architect who carried out the alterations to the royal property of Frogmore in the Home Park. Pugin branded him 'Wyatt the Destroyer', but his knighted nephew deserved the epithet much more on account of what he destroyed at Windsor Castle. The work with which he replaced the old buildings is not inspired; its mechanical masonry is unsympathetic; its battlements and defensive loopholes are not in the least romantic; its mouldings and details are clumsy and at close view it has been cleverly described as 'an enlarged toy fort.' Nevertheless it must be granted that the distant view of the whole, especially from the other side of the river above the bridge, is impressive.

The upper part of the Round Tower, which dominates the composition, is a part of Wyatville's work and is an ingenious piece of construction. It does not overburden the old foundations but is built up on new foundations within the old, so making two structures look like one with their unifying flint facing. Within the tower hangs a great bell captured during the Crimean War and tolled only at a Sovereign's death. The Round Tower was called the Rose Tower long ago because it was indeed of that colour, as accounts of the Castle written in the time of Edward III reveal—an interesting reminder of the Middle Age custom of painting, and even decorating, buildings externally in bright colours; a cheerful idea, no doubt picked up in Byzantium by the Crusaders.

There is much more to the Castle than Wyatville's structure and it should certainly be visited. We have already seen when

89

and why the place was first created by William the Conqueror. Now nothing earlier than Henry II's period is visible. Henry III added much, including the Curfew or Clewer Tower dominating Thames Street, but it was the romantic Edward III, born at Windsor, who turned it into a grand backcloth for chivalric pageantry, employing as clerks of works, first William of Wykeham and later Geoffrey Chaucer. Here Henry founded the Order of the Garter and built the original central tower to contain the Round Table for their meetings. Queen Elizabeth added the Gallery and the famous North Terrace which provides a grand panorama of the river.

Many fine things can be seen amongst the confusion of *bric-à-brac* in the State Apartments—Gobelins tapestries, finely wrought armour (including a suit of Henry VIII), furniture of many periods and a wealth of paintings by Rembrandt, Van Dyck, Rubens, Holbein and others. That remarkable model called the Queen's Doll's House is to be seen here, too. It was designed by Sir Edwin Lutyens and originally shown at the Wembley Exhibition in 1924-5.

Edward IV built the famous and wonderful ST. GEORGE'S CHAPEL which became the place of worship for the royal Order and the mausoleum of kings. Here lies buried the dust of Edward IV, Henry VI, Henry VIII, Charles I, William IV and the third, fourth, fifth and sixth Georges. East of the main chapel is a smaller one built by Henry VIII but lavishly redecorated as a memorial to the Prince Consort by Sir Gilbert Scott. In the vault beneath lies another royal body—that of Edward VII.

The inside of St. George's Chapel is magnificent, largely on account of the splendid fan vaulting of Henry VII's period, seen at its best from the aisles. Banners of the Knights of the Garter hanging above the carved 15th-century stalls of the choir make a soft and colourful foil to the monochrome of the hard stonework, while on the wall below the clerestory a delicately carved cornice of angels gives a binding strength to the whole. The stained glass is interesting. The great west window contains seventy-five figures of saints, popes and kings, fifty-one of which are of the 16th century, eighteen of the 18th century and six of about 1840. This chapel with its choir school, its deans' and canons' residencies and its Horse Shoe Cloisters has been said to be the nearest thing to a cathedral that Berkshire possesses.

In WINDSOR TOWN itself there is little to see except the Guild, or Town, Hall which was begun from designs by Sir Thomas Fitz in 1687 and completed by Sir Christopher Wren in 1713. It is of red brick and Portland stone and has that homely, human quality combined with monumentality which is so characteristic of Wren's work. Though it is in fact unlike anything that was ever built in Holland, it possesses, nevertheless a curiously Dutch character. At one end is a niche containing a statue of Queen Anne and at the other a good one of her consort, Prince George of Denmark, presented by Wren's son in 1713. Down the centre of the hall is a row of six sturdy columns inserted when the burgesses complained that the building was unstable. Wren did not agree with them; neither did he argue. He gave them their pillars but contemptuously made them an inch short of the beam they apparently support.

Wren has other associations with Windsor than the Town Hall. His father was Dean here and he was himself elected M.P. for the Borough in 1689. Moreover he prepared a grand scheme for reconstructing the Castle which was never carried out. Down near the bridge is a hotel called The Old House, which is said to have been his residence built to his own design. It has a pleasing symmetrical façade on which hangs a plaque stating that 'This house was built and occupied by Sir Christopher Wren, 1676'.

Among the best things of Windsor, to the author's taste, are the painted royal coats of arms suspended above a number of the shops in the main street. They are proudly displayed 'By Appointment' puffs and make, at the same time, gay street decorations. Near the river there is something else to look at—two large basins set on low plinths on each side of a monument to George V of bold, simple, strong design by Sir Edwin Lutyens.

To the east of the Castle, outside the town lies the HOME PARK which we passed on our way up. The North part of this park is always open to the public as WINDSOR PARK is also of course—that great area converted into a park from wild hunting forest by Charles II and later beautified by the Prince Regent. Most of Home Park is still the private property of the

King and here Prince Albert created a model farm. It contains a delightful 18th-century mansion called FROGMORE which George III turned into a kind of Petit Trianon for his Queen Charlotte in 1792. Though the stucco stables with their two domes remain from the original early 18th-century building, the main house was converted by James Wyatt in Greek Revival style for George III. Wyatt added a colonnade of Doric columns to the garden front and in the garden, laid out by Uvedale Price in the picturesque manner of the period at about the same time, Wyatt added a little Gothik ruin by the side of an artificial river. In the garden also stands a fantastic edifice in lavish German taste—a mausoleum to the Prince Consort built in 1861 and said to have cost £200,000. As Messrs. Piper and Betjeman express it so vividly in their *Murray's Berkshire Guide*, 'the Queen's grief still sobs through its interior as though she had left her sorrow on earth to haunt this rich, forbidding temple to her loneliness.' Unfortunately Frogmore is open to the public only on a few days of the year.

Down to WINDSOR BRIDGE now and across the river to the long street of ETON, which is the *ton* by the *eau*, the settlement by the water. Take a quick look at the bridge. It is not lovely, but it is interesting as a fairly early piece of cast ironwork, having been built in 1824. Another pleasing example of cast iron can be seen half way down the street of Eton on the right hand side—a very early Victorian pillar box in the form of a Doric column. The author has discovered only two others from the same mould anywhere else in England—both at Warwick.

Before long we reach the main group of buildings and the oldest part of ETON COLLEGE, founded in 1441 by Henry VI as a charitable institution. Then it was endowed to serve 'ten sad priests, four lay clerks, six choiristers, twenty-five grammar-scholars, and twenty-five poor men to pray for the king.' Now some 1,200 boys are educated here by no less than eighty masters and innumerable old customs and taboos.

One of the first things you notice in the group of old colour-ful buildings is a small statue under an elaborate canopy facing the street from the wall of the famous chapel. It represents William of Wayneflete, the first headmaster of Eton, who brought six boys from the cathedral at Winchester to form a nucleus for the new school (for Winchester School is the older).

The first quadrangle called School Yard is entered through a building called Upper School, built to Wren's designs in 1665 during the reign of William III. In the centre of this yard stands a bronze statue of the founder, Henry VI, erected in 1719, while on the right rises the famous school chapel. Though never quite completed according to intention and though greatly restored during the last century, its fine, soaring buttresses make it one of the best examples of the Perpendicular we possess, built at a time when Gothic engineering was nearing its technical peak.

To the east of School Yard is Lupton's Tower dating from 1520 and reminding one of Hampton Court and St. James's Palace with its bay windows, turrets and rich, decorated brickwork. Passing under the tower we come to the second quadrangle called Green Yard or Cloister Court, smaller and more intimate with its cloister of 1450 enclosing a lawn. Around this are grouped the College Hall, the venerable library and the houses of the Provost, Headmaster and Fellows.

If you happen to be at Eton on June the Fourth, you will see something of the College's famous annual festival, which is held as a Speech Day in memory of George III's birthday—a great event on the river, especially for the Wet Bobs of the school, with the procession of boats, the donning of strange, old naval uniforms by members of the crews, the parental visitations, the guzzling of strawberries and, as the night settles, the thrill of soaring, bursting rockets.

Above Windsor Bridge we pass on our right the wide open field of BROCAS from where the Castle looks its best. Under another railway bridge, round the racecourse and we pass Athens, the bathing place of Eton boys who, unless the water is now too polluted, may perhaps be seen taking elegant headers off the mound known as the Acropolis. A somewhat bleak reach follows until we come to BOVENEY LOCK and rollers. The lock is a charming one, especially in lilac time and it is enhanced by the simple wooden footbridge spanning the rollers—an excellent example of the timber vernacular of the Thames Conservancy, which has already been eulogised.

Just above the lock we obtain a good view of the distant Castle through a clearing in a belt of trees which someone has thoughtfully cut away to give you a picturesque *coup d'œil*. On the right

93

here little BOVENEY CHURCH lies cosily in a nest of thick, tall trees. It is very simple with its square bell tower of timber, and it is also very old, the walls being Norman and over three feet thick. Inside is a font of the 13th century, a few 16th-century benches and 17th-century wall panelling.

From here for nearly four miles up to, and beyond, Bray, the river is typically verdant and unspoiled. We first bear round a sharp bend to the right, keeping well clear of the shallows on the inside of the curve and we soon pass on the left two great mansions. The first is the huge turreted Victorian affair of OAKLEY COURT. Is it ugly? We would have said so once, and yet time alters our tastes, and have we a right to damn such Gothic romances, we who can produce buildings that are neither ugly nor beautiful but merely dull? At least Oakley Court has a robustness and the courageous character of its convictions. The garden with its generous lawn, its boathouse fantasy and its thick, carefully planted trees adds to the powerful atmosphere of the whole place.

The second big house is DOWN PLACE, a Georgian mansion which has curiously combined the rival styles of Classic and Gothic—or should one spell it Gothik to denote the earlier, more graceful and lighthearted of the two Gothic Revival phases? This is not a major monument but it is interesting in having been the residence of Jacob Tonson, the celebrated bookseller of the 18th century and friend of the great Whigs of his time—men like Walpole, Congreve, Addison, Steele, members of the Kitkat Club, whose formation was first suggested at a convivial meeting here. The consumption by its members of the excellent mutton pies of one Christopher Catt gave the name to this club, whose secretary Tonson became. Under the cover of joviality mixed with literary discussion, its real purpose was the defence of the House of Hanover.

Beyond QUEEN'S AIT, we can moor by the towpath on the right and take a short walk into Buckinghamshire to see the manor of DORNEY COURT and its attendant small church. The manor—the seat of the Palmers, a very old family of Saxon origin—is of timber frame with brick infilling dating from the early 16th century and it contains a hall with dais and screens —that great communal type of room which has degenerated in our modern homes into a mere downstairs entrance lobby and passage way. They say that the first pineapple produced in England was grown at Dorney Court. It was presented to Charles II and the event was recorded by the carving in wood of a pineapple in one of the rooms. The church is delightful, especially within. The brick tower is of 1530 and the porch and chapel are of Wren's period. Inside are some 16th-century seats, a pulpit and musicians' gallery of the 17th century, a font of the 12th century, a good monument of 1625 to Sir William Garrard, his wife and fifteen children, and the remains of a Gothic fresco of the Annunciation.

Just above Queen's Ait, lies MONKEY ISLAND, the most interesting of the Thames islands on account of the buildings there. One of these is a small hotel where you can obtain refreshments of every kind, including tea on its wide lawn. The aura of *al fresco* festivity has persisted here through at least two centuries. Many royal and noble people visited the place at one time or another even during this century, and in the hotel hangs an Edwardian photograph of a regal luncheon party held here in the open under the trees. The bearded face of King Edward VII dominates the gathering and by him sits his young grandson, now the Duke of Windsor, looking very solemn in a sailor suit.

Most of the hotel building is early Victorian but the central part is much older, having been built for the third Duke of Marlborough as a fishing lodge—some say, without any evidence, to designs by Vanbrugh who built Blenheim for the first Duke. The outside of this part is built of wood blocks to look like cut stone and inside is a coved ceiling decorated with 18th-century paintings by a Frenchman called Clermont, which depict monkeys in the dress of the period burlesquing various human occupations. One naturally supposes that the name of the island derives from this *syngerie*, but Thacker suggests reasonably that it comes from Monks Ey, the name given to the island when it belonged to a monastery.

The other building to the east is now a private house; part of it is quite modern, part Victorian and part 18th-century. You may have noticed the pretty classical elevation of the oldest part closing the view as we came upstream. This was also built for the third Duke of Marlborough as a pavilion with open sides on the ground floor (now closed in) and a banqueting hall above. This latter room is splendidly decorated with finely

F   95 detailed fireplace and panelling. Above is elaborate plaster-work along the frieze and on the ceiling of water sprites, mermaids, sea serpents and other devices. Today all this is pure white but originally it was splendidly coloured with a background of dark green against which the figures stood out in shining gold leaf. *Murray's Berkshire Guide* says that this Temple may be either by Charles Stanley or Roberts of Oxford of a date round about 1725 but this author suggests that the architect may equally well have been the renowned William Kent (1684-1748), the protégé of Lord Burlington, architect of Holkham Hall, furniture designer, decorator, portrait painter, Yorkshireman, who with enormous enthusiasm, energy and ability worked his way up to fame as an architect from apprenticeship to a coach painter. The fire-place details and the plaster work are in the Kent manner. More telling still is the rather heavy detailing of the ceiling which has a Jacobean feeling, and as we saw at Hampton Court Kent did go in for Jacobean Revival plasterwork.

The stream at Monkey Island is narrow and the current is strong almost as far as BRAY LOCK, but just beyond Amerden Priory (formerly an hotel and a very long time before that a priory whose moat can still be seen as a dell among the trees) the river opens up to give a pleasant, wide view towards the weir and the cottage and gates of the lock. On the left by the weir stands a typical 18th-century, white weather-boarded mill, now converted into a delightful private home, like a number of others of its kind on the river. There has been a mill at this spot at least since the Domesday Survey.

Bray Lock is among the most pleasing of all the pleasing locks of the Thames, largely on account of the gardening skill of the present keeper, Mr. Baldwin, who won the big cup in 1950 for the best lock garden of the river. It has that informal, flower-filled character of the English cottage garden which is so much more sympathetic and human than the rigid perfection of a geometric lay-out.

Beyond Headpile Eyot on the left lies BRAY which should certainly be visited. It has a villagey charm in spite of its sophisticated, arty-crafty, cosmopolitan, expensive week-end atmosphere purveyed by the false half-timbering of many of the cottages and by the *Hotel de Paris* and the *Hind's Head Hotel*, so justly renowned for its good food and wine.

Yes, Sir, this is the Vicar's Bray, though the popular ballad (quite likely composed by one of the wits who visited Tonson at Down Place) is not correct in its dates. In his *Worthies of England* (1662) Fuller records that:

The vivacious vicar thereof, living under King Henry VIII, King Edward VI, Queen Mary, and Queen Elizabeth, was first a Papist, then a Protestant, then a Papist, then a Protestant again. He had seen some martyrs burnt at Windsor, and found this fire too hot for his tender temper. This vicar being taxed by one for being a turncoat and an inconstant changeling—'Not so', said he, 'for I always kept my principle which is this—to live and die the Vicar of Bray.'

How much more comfortable than to suffer the ghastly deaths of those whose names are recorded in John Fox's *Book of Martyrs,* a tattered volume of which is still preserved in Bray Church.

There is another Vicar of Bray story, and one less well known, 'for the truth of which I cannot vouch', as Samuel Ireland puts it in his Thames commentary of 1791. He gives the story thus:

Charles the Second had been hunting in Windsor Forest, and in the chase was separated from his attendants. In returning he lost his road, and came to Bray after it was dark, where, on enquiring for the Vicar's house, and being introduced, he told him that he was a traveller who had lost his way, and having spent all his money, begged that he would render him assistance to proceed on his journey, and that he would soon repay him with the greatest honesty. The Vicar told him he was an impostor, and bade him go out of his house with great rudeness. But the Curate (who was with the vicar) said that he pitied the traveller, and lent him a little money. The King then disclosed who he was, and upbrading the Vicar for his inhumanity, said, 'The Vicar of Bray shall be Vicar of Bray still, but the Curate shall be Canon of Windsor';—and it is said that the King made his word good.

The story has several versions, one of which gives James I as the king concerned.

The square tower of the church helps to make a very pretty picture, especially when seen above the trees from the river. Part of the church is about 1300 but the tower, chancel and chapels date from about 1500 and the whole was greatly 'restored' in the middle of the last century. Inside are some interesting brasses and a good alabaster monument on the north wall with effigies of William Goddard and his wife, Joyce

Mauncell. Goddard's hands rest on a skull, showing that the monument was erected after his death in 1609. He was the founder of Jesus Hospital in Bray.

Outside the church at the south-east corner of the church-yard is a half-timbered gatehouse of the early 15th century, which was probably at one time the Chantry House built for the parish clergyman. On one of the timbers is the date 1448 which may be the year of its erection.

At the other end of the village stands the village hall. It is a distinguished building in that it must be the ugliest village hall in the world. Thereby it serves as a foil to the dignity and beauty of the JESUS HOSPITAL almshouses just beyond. The founder's painted statue stands in a niche over the entrance above his own coat of arms and those of the Fishmongers' Company of which he was a free brother. He gave clear in-structions in his will about the building of the almshouses, which, as you can see, were faithfully carried out—'the outer walls to be built of brick—there shall be rooms with chimneys fit and convenient for 40 poor people to dwell in—a chapel to serve Almighty God for ever—to be called Jesus Hospital in Bray of the foundation of William Goddard.' Work on the place was begun in 1623 and possibly those tall, clipped evergreens lining the front were planted at that time. The courtyard is dominated at the end by the contemporary chapel, whose interior was entirely gutted in recent years but then excellently renewed. The courtyard with its small trees and its garden plots tended by the inhabitants, formed the setting for Frederick Walker's well-known painting *The Harbour of Refuge,* an apt title for the place which purveys a wonderful sense of tranquil retreat.

From Bray to MAIDENHEAD is about a mile. This reach is wide and shallow and therefore good for punting. On the left large Edwardian mansions and mature gardens line the bank, several not without character, and as you pass them you can play a guessing game, trying to pick out the lawn where Mrs. Langtry, the beautiful, redhaired Jersey Lily of the Edwardian stage, once held court. Ahead lies the red brick railway bridge of the former Great Western Railway framing Maidenhead's elegant stone bridge, built to designs by Sir Robert Taylor in 1772. The railway bridge, of red engineering brickwork, is by far the best of all the Thames railway bridges, and was built by Sir Isambard Brunel in the late 1830s. It has the two widest, and at the same time flattest, pure brick arch spans in the world—128 feet wide with a rise of only 24 feet.

And here is Maidenhead, or at least the riverside part of it, for the main town is about a mile away to the west. Maidenhead is an old market town with very little history and almost no distinctions except a pleasing row of old brick almshouses of 1659 lying on the main road between the bridge and the town. The name Maidenhead is variously supposed to derive from the hythe, or wharf, in the meadow; the Magne hithe, or large wharf; Mai dun hythe or wharf at the great hill (of Taplow); the mid hythe between Windsor and Reading. Another, somewhat visionary, suggestion is that the name comes from the association with the head of a British maiden, which was here revered, the girl being one of the eleven thousand virgins said to have been martyred with St. Ursula on the banks of the Rhine near Cologne. That is a very large number and a Jesuit named Simordus, judging that the meeting together of so many virgins was improbable, has thoughtfully reduced the number to two.

Along past the moored cruisers and the boats for hire, past the string of islands on the right which shroud some industrial buildings, and we reach Boulter's Lock. From here as far as Sonning, the river will be at its most enchanting all the way.

5

Maidenhead to Reading

A BOULTER IS A MILLER. Hence the name of the most famous lock on the river, for an old mill stands on the lock island here. BOULTER'S LOCK was the first and the lowest on the river of the first set of eight to be built under the legislation of 1770. As you see it today, however, the works date only from 1912. To cope with the heavy pleasure traffic which reaches its annual peak on Ascot Sunday, it has been built with two compartments, or rather with one large compartment, the upper end of which can be shut off by a pair of gates to deal with normal situations when only a few small craft are passing through. This saves both time and water.

While these new works at Boulter's were being constructed Fred Thacker was here, for he muses in his *Thames Highway:*

I roamed and dreamed over Ray Mill close one day of March in 1912 . . . and discerned before it was too late what a little kingdom the island once formed for the soul and the hand of man. At the lower end was his material living, the mill busy enough in old centuries when England was wise to feed herself; and close by stood his home. Here lay all his intercourse with the outer world. Within lay secluded what an earthly paradise, surrounded with living Thames. Still I beheld shady undulating alleys leading by little bridges across artificial brooks; still ancient barns and bowers of honeysuckle and clematis; still tiny sandy capes and bays where, a long lifetime ago, you might have sat golden hours and watched the last Thames salmon leap below the weir . . . A memory of Boulter's this which compensates for all the alien things of Maidenhead.

Once along the narrow water-lane above the lock the intruding motor road on the Berkshire side departs and the fine CLIVEDEN REACH opens out before us. On the right rise the woods thick with trees of every kind, many no doubt descendants from the primeval forest which once covered this land.

High up on the hill ahead CLIVEDEN COURT itself comes into view, impressive at first sight but regarded more closely a rather dull and pompous piece of classicism. All the same, it is well worth visiting on one of those days when the public are admitted. The original house which stood here was built by the dissolute Carolean courtier, George Villiers, Second Duke of Buckingham, during the 17th century—the fellow of whom Dryden wrote so scathingly:

> A man so various, that he seem'd to be
> Not one, but all mankind's epitome . . .
> Who in the course of one revolving moon,
> Was chemist, fiddler, statesman and buffoon;
> Then all for women, painting, fiddling, drinking,
> Besides a thousand freaks that died in thinking.

This house passed to the Earl of Orkney, Marlborough's companion in arms, and was later occupied by Frederick, Prince of Wales, father of George III. The Duke of Buckingham's architect was a William Wynne and part of his work, though somewhat altered, still stands. This consists of the *Insanae Substructiones* of about 1670, the great underbuilding of the terrace, over 400 feet long and 25 feet wide, which overlooks the Thames valley. The house was destroyed by fire in 1795 but was rebuilt in the first half of the 19th century by Sir George Warrender who sold it to the Duke of Sutherland. Another great fire occurred in 1849 after which the present house was built by the Duke to designs by Sir Charles Barry, architect of the Houses of Parliament. It became the seat of the Duke of Westminster and then the American millionaire, Mr. William Waldorf Astor, bought it. To the Astors (remember their Cliveden Set?) it still partly belongs—partly, because in 1942 Lord Astor gave much of the estate to the National Trust, while retaining the right to live there. To cut down cost, the façades of the house were not built of stone but were faced with cement of a depressing colour and texture. The campanile and the stable block were added in 1861 and are not Barry's work. A thing of beauty in front of the house is the fine balustrade with fountains, stone seats and boldly carved panels which originally stood in the gardens of the Villa Borghese. The statues on the piers, however, are not an intrinsic part of the Italian balustrade but are French.

Below Cliveden crosses the first of the three ferries linking the towpath which leads to Cookham. It has the pleasing and mysterious name of MY LADY FERRY, which may be a corruption of the old local place name of Is-lade. Above the ferry is the wooded FORMOSA ISLAND, the largest on the river at over 50 acres. Upon it, amidst a damp tangle of undergrowth which was once the well-tended garden of a baronet, stand the ruins of an 18th-century villa, which have a sad and picturesque attraction.

Through the delightful lock and cut of COOKHAM we reach the low bridge of wood and cast iron built in 1867 for the surprisingly modest sum of £2,520—a white, light, utilitarian structure, not without grace, which provides one more example to show how rash it is to damn all Victorian design as 'ugly'. The octagonal brick toll cottage on the Buckinghamshire end is attractive and of earlier date than the bridge. It was used by the toll keeper right up to 1947 when the local council took over the bridge from the private owners and toll collecting came to an end here. Now (1951) tolls are paid only on two bridges of the Thames—at Whitchurch and Swinford. Toll collecting was often a paying proposition. At Cookham, for instance, as the author learned from the tenant of the cottage, the last collector paid an annual rent of £350 to the owners of the bridge. Whatever else he collected above that sum during the year was his to keep. Since on a busy day, such as a Regatta day, he could take as much as £20, he retired with a modest fortune.

Cookham is a relatively unspoiled village, mentioned as a market town in the *Domesday Book* and having associations with Charles II and Nell Gwynne. It has an old church, partly Norman, partly Early English, with a fine square tower of flint built in the 16th century. In the centre of the village is a curious boulder, possibly a meteorite, called the Tarry Stone said to have been used up to the end of the 16th century on the Moor (as the green is called) in connection with traditional village games.

Before leaving Cookham glance back down stream, where the waters divide into three. The picture is enchanting, especially when the sun lights up the elegant white hulls of the little ships moored in the Odney backwater and a group of swans glides quietly through the dark water.

The SWANS, which give much to the charm of the river, have an interesting history. The owning of swans on any English river has always been a privilege. These birds have for centuries survived under strong legal protection and have enjoyed the status of a sort of royal heraldic totem. Punishment for stealing swans or their eggs, or for driving away the birds during breeding time, has always been heavy; in the *Order for Swannes* of 1570, for instance, it is laid down that those who erase or counterfeit any owner's marks on a bird shall be imprisoned for a year. In the reign of Edward IV no one who did not possess a freehold valued at least at five marks was allowed to keep swans and it was then ordained that on every river all had to be examined, counted and recorded. Henry VIII instituted the marking of cygnets with nicks on the beaks and any swan not marked automatically became Crown property.

Swans are believed to have been introduced into England from Cyprus by Richard I in the 12th century. For some time only those of royal or noble blood were permitted to keep them, but later the City Companies, among others, received the concession to do so at a time when English trade was becoming important and beginning to rival that of the Low Countries. Today on the Thames all the swans belong either to the King or to the Dyers' and the Vintners' Companies of London. The old yearly ceremony of Swan Upping or Swan Hopping still takes place when the young birds are 'upped' from the water for examination and marking by the King's Swan-Keeper and the Swan Masters of the two City Companies, a ceremony which has hardly changed during four centuries. Once a year in July or August a small and colourful fleet of boats sets out from Southwark Bridge in gay panoply. Flags fly and the Masters' assistants are dressed in striped jerseys and tasselled caps, while the King's Swan-Keeper wears a scarlet coat. Since the Crown has about 500 swans, the Dyers 65 and the Vintners 45, the upping takes about a week. It is a tough kind of picnic, as anyone who has had close contact with this handsome but aggressive bird will appreciate, and it concludes with a traditional banquet held at a river-side inn when the *pièce de résistance* is a dish of succulent swan's meat.

The markings used today consist of one small nick under the right side of the bill for the Dyers' birds and two nicks on either side for the Vintners' (hence the tavern sign of *The Swan with Two Necks* i.e. nicks). Since 1910 the King's birds have been left unmarked. Marking is therefore simple now but a hundred years ago is was much more interesting, thus:

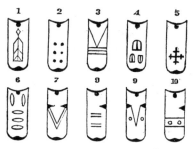

1. Eton College
2. Queen of Charles I
3. Charles I
4. Cambridge
5. Oxford
6. Queen Victoria
7. Vintners' Company (modern mark)
8. Dyers' Company (modern mark)
9. Vintners' Company (ancient mark)
10. Dyers' Company (ancient mark)

Swan marks

Dickens records in his *Dictionary of the Thames* that the old marks were simplified in 1878 after the Society for the Prevention of Cruelty to Animals had prosecuted the swanherds employed by the Crown and the two City Companies. The Society protested that the cutting of the upper mandible and the stopping of the slight bleeding with pitch was painful to the birds, but it lost the case.

Swan Upping has for a long time been regarded in a festive spirit. A letter written by a man called Barnes to another called Hewett dated August 12, 1780, gives one charming vignette of this ancient river ceremony (and incidentally proves that houseboats are older than either the Edwardian or even the Victorian days). The letter reads:

I was all yesterday on the most cheerful water party up the river, as high as Sunbury. At Richmond we were fortunate in overtaking Mr. Sharp's barge (or his country house, which has every accommodation of beds, etc.), and also the Navigation barge with my Lord and Lady Mayoress, etc., going the boundaries of the river, which drew people of all ranks down to the water-side. As I believe they call it Swanhopping season, all the gardens next the river are lined with ladies and gentlemen to see the show and hear the music, which brings down all the belles to shew off.

Up a wide reach and past BOURNE END, a bungalow resort of little interest, we come to the Upper Thames Sailing Club. Notice a fine old ship's figurehead on the lawn here. Beyond Bourne End the countryside is open on both sides until we come to two islands. If we keep to the left of them we shall pass a high bluff covered with the first trees of the magnificent Quarry Woods which decorate the landscape to the south-east of Marlow. After a turn to the right and a struggle up against a swift race we reach the MARLOW LOCK with its weather-boarded mill.

Above the lock one of the prettiest scenes on the river faces us—at its best when the evening sunlight glitters in the long weir curving to the *Compleat Angler Hotel,* and makes a silhouette of the church spire rising above the low, ephemeral sweep of the suspension bridge. On the right, pleasing Georgian houses lie back behind lawns and weeping willow trees.

GREAT MARLOW is of Saxon origin and was for a long time an important market town, dependent to a great extent on the river. From here the bone-lace made in the town, brass kettles and pans from the Temple Mills upstream, the malt and grain from High Wycombe, beech wood from Buckinghamshire were loaded onto barges plying to London. And there was also much water carriage up-stream from London. In 1767, for example, over 56,000 tons of merchandise passed up through the flash lock here—a fair amount for those days. Yet many navigational difficulties had to be faced and continual complaints have been recorded, apart from the usual ones rising from the conflicts between boaters and millers concerning the supply of water for the flashes. For instance, then (as now) there was no towpath between the bridge and the lock so that towlines of the fantastic length of a quarter of a mile had to be wielded.

Today Marlow is a quiet little town except during the gay spell of the yearly Regatta, and, thanks to its being served only by a branch line, it has retained much of its Georgian dignity. The atmosphere of the place is happy and relaxed as though every day were a Saturday.

The most remarkable structure in the town is the small suspension bridge. It was started in 1829 by John Millington, but he went off to America and the work was completed by William Tierney Clark to his own design in 1832. Clark is less well known than he deserves to be, for, apart from his feat at Marlow, he designed the first Hammersmith Suspension Bridge (replaced in 1885) and also the famous bridge which still links Buda with Pest. Most of the Thames bridges are conventional in having been designed to be seen from the sides; the approach views show nothing more exciting than a hump in the road between balustrades. Marlow Bridge when built was new and different for it attained economically, by the use of iron combined with stone, an effect that had been sought by constructors for a long time—the monumental approach, the grand entrance. With its two heavy stone pylons pierced by triumphal, classic arches which contrast powerfully with the delicate, white-painted ironwork, it is a little beauty—an example of that period when engineering and architecture enjoyed a brief but happy marriage. Apart from its good design *per se,* the bridge rounds off the charm of the whole town and forms an excellent foil to the spire of the Gothic Revival tower rising near by.

The church, of yellow brick dressed with stone, was entirely rebuilt in 1834 by a London architect, Charles Inwood, and was remodelled in the 1870's by J. Oldrid Scott. It is a poor example of the late Gothic Revival but it is the kind of building for which one acquires an inexplicable affection in spite of its shortcomings, and it has the advantage of being well placed in the landscape. Inside are a number of monuments preserved from the earlier church. One of the more interesting, though a crude piece of work, is the wall monument to Sir Miles Hobart, which hangs in the lobby. He was that Speaker of the House of Commons who, during a memorable debate on tonnage and poundage in 1628, locked the door of the House and kept the key in his pocket until the resolutions were passed. He was killed in 1636 when the wheel of his coach broke on Snow Hill, Holborn, and the coach overturned—an event depicted in a small bas-relief at the base of his monument, which was paid for by Parliament.

In the vestry hangs a portrait of The Spotted Boy, the young negro from the Caribbean, whom John Richardson, the famous showman, exhibited with considerable financial benefit round the country. Richardson was born in the workhouse at Marlow and was buried in the churchyard here, being laid at his own request beside his Spotted Boy, who had died in 1812—a pathetic little fellow, one imagines, who had enjoyed but eight years of bewildering life.

Two other ecclesiastical buildings are worth inspecting in Marlow. The first is the Congregational Chapel of 1840 built in yellow brick and a good sample of the simple nonconformist tradition. It cost only £1,050 and it is obvious that the Congregationalists obtained much better value for their money than the parishioners whose church consumed £15,000 in the erection. The second is the Roman Catholic church designed without inspiration by A. W. N. Pugin (famed for his Gothic detailing in the Houses of Parliament) and built about 1845 at the time of the Catholic Revival. It has a broach spire, a type found often in the Midland villages but rarely in the Thames Valley. The church possesses a famous relic said to be the mummified hand of St. James the Apostle, which, having suffered a number of adventures in Europe during the Middle Ages, was brought to England. Henry I presented it to Reading Abbey. At the Dissolution it was lost but was found again in the 17th century during digging for the foundations of Reading Gaol. Then it seems to have found its way to Danesfield, a great house we shall pass higher up river. Its owner was a Catholic who presented the relic to the Catholic church at Marlow, where, let us hope, since it has not been permitted to die a natural death, it may at least enjoy eternal rest.

The best possessions of Marlow are the Georgian houses, notably Marlow Place just by the cinema, which is said to have been built in 1720 for George II when Prince of Wales. Because of the curious baroque ornamentation of the capitals of the pilasters at the angles of the house and of the main doorway, as well as other features such as the bold cornice under the pediment, it has been surmised that the architect was the famous Thomas Archer. Another good example is Remnantz in West Street with its fine brick gate-piers and cupola over the stables—a house which was taken over as the Junior Branch of the Royal Military College from 1802 until 1811. Next to it stands Weston House with a handsome shell hood of moulded plasterwork over the doorway and a charming gazebo overlooking the road.

In the High Street the carved wooden doorway of the post office provides an example of the high standard of detailing in the 18th century even among local builders, who kept abreast of the fashion by the free use of the many architectural pattern-books available at that time. The most charming house in the High Street, however, is No. 72, the white stucco building half way up on the left. It has two quadrant bays and the exquisite detailing of its period when refined, educated building in England was singing its swan song.

The High Street vista is closed at its upper end by the Market House, now the *Crown Inn,* a building which replaced the old timber market-house during the 18th-century, and is now rather disfigured. It is often stated that the designer was James Wyatt, Surveyor-General at the time of its construction, but it is far more likely that his less famous brother, Samuel Wyatt (1737-1807), was the architect. For one thing Samuel had just completed Temple House for the local M.P. which stood a mile up-river by the Temple Mills (pulled down in the 1930s). For another, Samuel added to these mills and the cupola on them closely resembles that which we now see above the Market House, whose general character is, in any case, not up to James's standard.

The reach from Marlow to Temple Lock is in no way dramatic and yet has a strange appeal which is difficult to analyse. The appeal is no doubt partly due to the sense of calm continuity of time given by the church and Abbey of Bisham which stand close to the water among the trees on the Berkshire side.

Behind them lies the picturesque brick village of BISHAM, of Saxon origin and once known as Bustleham. The square tower of the church is 12th-century but apart from this and the 16th-century chapel, the whole was virtually rebuilt in Victorian times. Nevertheless we must certainly moor by the churchyard and enter the church, for its chapel contains some fine, rare monuments, outstanding treasures of the river. It is called the Hoby Chapel (pronounced Hobby), the Hobys being the local lords from the time of the Dissolution right up to the 18th century. The first of their monuments you notice is a little, free-standing affair of 1605 backed by a superb armorial window of six lights, dated 1609. This, called the Swan Monument, consists of a stone pyramid surmounted by a flaming red heart at the base of which are four swans with wings outstretched. It was erected by Sir Edward Hoby, son of the Elizabeth who built the chapel, and is dedicated to his wife Margaret. She was born a Cary, whose family crest was a swan. Against the wall south of the Swan Monument, stands the beautifully wrought alabaster Tomb of the Two Knights, the half-brothers, Sir Philip and Sir Thomas Hoby, which was erected by Elizabeth, the latter's wife.

The monument to Lady Elizabeth herself is the magnificent, elaborate, coloured one with a canopy standing further west. This aunt of Francis Bacon kneels at a prayer desk with her seven children around her. She wears a ruff, a stomacher and a wonderful coif surmounted by a coronet. Her face, though refined and intelligent, is cruel. A legend relates that she beat one of her young sons to death for blotting his copy books. Her remorse was so great that she still haunts the neighbouring abbey, while before her floats a self-supporting bowl in which she tries hopelessly to wash her guilty hands. A peculiar thing about this ghost is that its tones are seen in reverse like a photographic negative, and a peculiar event which supports the legend is that in 1840 during alterations to the abbey, the workmen discovered some badly blotted copy books of the 16th century. She buried several of her children as well as two husbands (the second was Lord John Russell, who lies in Westminster Abbey)—a necrophilous soul who seems to have delighted in the ceremonies and trappings of death, even to the preparations for her own demise, which occurred when she was over eighty.

Above the church is the old vicarage and garden, and beyond that is BISHAM ABBEY, now a training college of the Central Council of Physical Recreation. It was founded in the reign of Stephen as a preceptory of Knights Templar, now remembered in the name, Temple Lock. In 1337 it became an Augustinian priory and in 1536, at the Dissolution, it was destroyed except for the porch and the great hall, which remain to this day. The present Tudor house was erected by Henry VIII who gave it to his 'great Flanders Mare', Anne of Cleves. Later she exchanged the place with Sir Philip Hoby for a manor in Kent. It is believed that Queen Elizabeth spent three years of her childhood at Bisham Abbey.

We pass on our left the old TEMPLE MILLS, now producing paper, but at one time famous for their copper ware. Defoe in his *Tour* of the early 18th century describes them as 'three very remarkable Mills, called the Temple-mills, for making Bisham Abbey Battery-work, viz. Brass Kettles and Pans etc. of all Sorts. And these works were attended with no small Success, till in the Year 1720, they made a Bubble of it; and then it ran the Fate of all the Bubbles at that time.' Brass and copper ware, nevertheless, was still being made here at least up to the 1790s.

TEMPLE LOCK is notable for its trim topiary and its grand chestnut trees. Above it lies a short but very beautiful reach to Hurley Lock and village. Here is a complex of islands and backwaters, the most inviting water being that which leads up to the weir past HARLEYFORD MANOR, a bold, square, rather bald-looking red brick building standing in well planted grounds. It was built for Sir Robert Clayton in 1755 by the architect Sir Robert Taylor (1714-1788), whose bridge we admired at Maidenhead. Though we shall find other examples of Taylor's work at Wallingford, not many of his buildings survive in their original state. He was, however, very successful and until Robert Adam came on the scene divided most of the important part of the practice of the profession in the country with James Paine. So successful was he that, though he inherited nothing, he left a fortune of £180,000, which he bequeathed for the foundation of the Taylorian Institute at Oxford for the study of modern languages. The son of a stonemason, he was apprenticed to Sir Henry Cheere, the sculptor, and himself worked as a sculptor for many years (the pediment of the Mansion House is his). He did not take up architecture until he was forty, but became architect to the Bank of England from 1765 until 1788, when he was succeeded by Sir John Soane. There he designed the Court Room and carried out some sculpture. He is known, too, for the Stone Buildings, Lincoln's Inn and for Ely House in Dover Street.

Harleyford Manor which must have been one of Taylor's first jobs, is in the standard Palladian mode—tidy and compact but now marred by the Victorian glazing and sashing of the widows. Mrs. Lybbe-Powys, a riverside dweller who kept a diary of her times, visited the new Manor in 1767 and admired its one innovation, the way in which 'the whole of the offices were so contrived in a pit, as to be perfectly invisible' —the pit being the forerunner of the depressing Victorian base-

ᴀʙᴏᴠᴇ, Boulter's Lock at Maidenhead on one of its busy days. The lock and narrow cut gives entrance to the grandest landscape of the river—the Cliveden Reach. On the right lies the lock cottage and the island where a mill wheel once turned (a boulter being a miller). ʀɪɢʜᴛ, the cottage at My Lady Ferry which crosses the upper end of the Cliveden Reach.

A September morning at Cliveden Woods. With its encroach-
ing trees and steep forested
slope giving a sense of enclosed
tropical wilderness, this is the
most dramatic reach of the
whole river and creates a strong
contrast to the flat, open spaces
which soon follow beyond
Cookham (see pages 120-1).
BELOW, a noble iron bollard
on the Berkshire bank at My
Lady Ferry.

ABOVE, members of the Upper Thames Sailing Club at
Bourne End prepare for a race on a windy day.
RIGHT, the figurehead of Neptune from the old battle-
ship *Vengeance* now surveys the lawn of the sailing club.
FACING PAGE, TOP, a camping party enjoys elevenses
on an island above Bourne End. BELOW, a romantic
riverside retreat of the Edwardian era, with its picturesque jumble of gables and balconies, is still well
preserved among the beeches of Quarry Woods.

FACING PAGE, TOP, a sumptuous motor boat moored below Marlow Bridge. BELOW, the landscape above Marlow looking downstream towards the elegant suspension bridge and its foil, the spire of Marlow Church. ABOVE, the lawn of the *Compleat Angler* at Marlow. RIGHT, the monumental approach to Marlow across the bridge.

Two of the finest church monuments along the river can be found in Bisham Church, both being of the early 17th century. FACING PAGE, the Swan Monument topped by a flaming red heart. ABOVE, detail of the monument to Lady Elizabeth Hoby and her seven children. LEFT, the rollers and topiary of Temple Lock; a shaft of evening sunlight catches the row of distant white posts so typical of the simple, but decorative, Thames trim.

119

LEFT, the open meadowland
of Oxfordshire between Hurley
and Hambleden gives strong
contrasting relief in landscape
along the river line to such enclosed reaches as that at Cliveden (pages 112-3). BELOW,
the Georgian manor of Harleyford by the weir stream near
Hurley Lock.

ABOVE, Hambleden Mill, one of the few mills on the river which still serve their first purpose, though water no longer provides its power. BELOW, the almshouses of 1830 facing Henley churchyard.

LEFT, rowing men at Henley Regatta. ABOVE, the Ragged Arches of Park Place built with stones from Reading Abbey. BELOW another charming Thames Conservancy footbridge, at Shiplake Lock.

The footbridge of timber which takes the towpath right out into the river above Marsh Lock. This gives an example of how the proposed Riverside Walk can be made interesting in spite of its level way.

RIGHT, the *Bull Inn* at Sonning, one of the many old buildings of a picturesque village. BELOW, Sonning's graceful bridge of mellow brickwork gives entrance to a short arboreal reach before Sonning Lock with its famous garden is reached. Part of our journey is over; the break of Reading and the anti-Thames lies ahead.

ment*. Though Harleyford belonged to the lord of the manor
and stands on the site of an earlier manor house, it is a typical
Cit's Country Box built at the time when the rich city merchants,
whose places of business and dwellings had hitherto been combined, were building country residences where they could take
on the status of landed gentlemen. As Robert Lloyd wrote in
his poem of 1757:

> The wealthy Cit, grown old in trade,
> Now wishes for the rural shade . . .
> And by th' approaching summer season,
> Draws a few hundreds from the stocks,
> And purchases his Country Box.

Opposite Harleyford lies HURLEY VILLAGE, very old and
having some interesting features but today unkempt and sullied
by an uncontrolled caravan encampment. Its *Old Bell Inn* is
of the 15th-century and, like its 14th-century tithe barn and
round dovecot—both of buttressed stone—originally belonged
to a Benedictine monastery. In Elizabeth's reign a mansion
called Lady Place was erected on the site of this monastery by Sir
Richard Lovelace from the spoils captured from Spanish gal-
leons. He was one of Sir Francis Drake's comrades and in the
manner of his time shaped the plan of his house in the form of
the letter E in honour of the Queen. Here John, Lord Lovelace,
plotted with his friends in the old Norman vaults beneath his
house for the 'calling in' of William of Orange. The house was
pulled down in 1837, but the original priory chapel still stands
as the village church. Part of the church is pre-Conquest though
the whole was much restored in the last century.

Beyond Hurley Lock some chalk bluffs rise up in the midst of
a colourful treescape. Two large houses stand high up on the
hill behind—the first a large, symmetrical neo-Georgian building with luxurious gardens, and the second the great mansion
of DANESFIELD of indeterminate style which was built at the
turn of the century on the site of a much older house. The archi-

---

*An innovation, that is, vis-à-vis the Palladian mansion which usually placed the
servants' quarters in side pavilions. Earlier Sir Roger Pratt had incorporated a
basement in his Coleshill House (completed in 1662) and this system was often
used thereafter in the Wren period, as at Wren's Fawley Court, which we shall
pass a few miles further on.

H

tect was F. H. Romaine-Walker, who used chalk from the local quarries as his material.

Beyond an island we pass on our right the fascinating house and garden known as MEDMENHAM ABBEY, which was originally a mere cell for Cistercian monks founded in 1204. At the Dissolution the commissioners reported that only two monks lived here 'who both desyren to go to houses of religion— servants none, woods none, debts none—bells etc. worth £2 1s. 8d'. What seem to be medieval ruins here now are, in fact, pieces of 18th-century picture making built with the old materials of the monastery but looking charming enough behind the lawn with its great elm and weeping willow. Otherwise the house is partly Elizabethan and partly modern. Sir Francis Dashwood, one of our Chancellors of the Exchequer, reconstructed the old place and here, dressed in robes of blue and crimson, the twelve members of his Hell Fire Club—that mysterious and diabolical order of 'Franciscan Monks'—met for their debauches from 1755 until 1762. No doubt the squalor of these orgiastic Black Magic meetings, reputed to have been held in this quiet spot, were exaggerated at the time and received undue publicity in that once popular, but now almost forgotten, romance, *Chrysal or The Adventures of a Guinea*. Most of these Medmenham Monks were, after all, men of learning, wit and sensibility who settled down later in life to distinguished careers. Probably the club provided an outlet for the hearty humour and horseplay of the period, because a legend relates that at one meeting of the so-called monks, after the enactment of certain profane rites which parodied those of their impecunious but debt-free predecessors, a member released a large monkey made up to resemble the Devil, which he had concealed in a chest. The shock to the assembly was considerable and after this, so it is said, no more meetings were held. Sir Francis himself, you may recall, also founded the Dilettante Club whose right of membership, according to Walpole, was to have visited Italy and to have been drunk. He also erected that strange golden ball on top of the tower of West Wycombe Church, where he would sit carousing with his boon companions, alternately conversing, sipping port and admiring the view. Local gossip says that Medmenham Abbey is haunted by some kind of vague monkish being whose presence is heralded by an intense and unpleasant chilliness in the air and by the terrified yelping of dogs.

Just above the Abbey on the same bank is a small boat house, a group of splendid poplars and a small monument surmounted by a cupid who points across the river. It looks like a village war memorial but its bronze plaque reads: 'This monument was erected to commemorate the successful action fought by Hudson Ewebank Kearley, First Viscount Devonport P.C. which resulted in the Court of Appeal deciding on the 28th March, 1899, that Medmenham Ferry is public.' Next to it stands a small tree also possessing a plaque. This one reads: 'Chestnut tree planted May 6 1935 to commemorate the silver jubilee of H.M. King George V.'

MEDMENHAM VILLAGE runs up from the river to the main road between Marlow and Henley. The village is beautifully kept—a pleasant discovery after the squalor of Hurley. The gardens are bright with flowers, the topiary is properly trimmed, the paintwork is fresh. The little modern post office and shop has been designed with simplicity and good taste. No dreary modern villas with asbestos roofs are permitted here. Nothing grates. The people smile at you and up at the corner the grass in the churchyard has been newly mown—a rare sight these days. It is like entering a very old but very refreshing world. The vicar, the Rev. Arthur Plaisted, who must love the place and its people and has written about Medmenham and the district in his *English Architecture in a Country Village,* probably deserves most of the credit for all this.

The church, partly late Norman, lies snugly in its dipping churchyard and looks pretty in its frame of chestnut trees. The chancel arch and roof are good examples of medieval carpentry but there is little else remarkable inside the church. Outside, standing against the east wall, are two very pleasing and well-preserved headstones carved in the 18th century.

For the next two miles up river nothing spoils the fertile landscape. First we pass MAGPIE ISLAND and if we can navigate the shallow left-hand stream, we shall discover there a cottage retreat with Gothik quatrefoil windows. It belongs to a writer and is like something you have pictured in your day-dreams of escape from the oppressive urban world. Then high up on the left the sturdy pedimented brick mansion of CULHAM COURT

built in 1771 comes into view, not unlike Harleyford, but rather
better in design. Here the Hon. F. West, son of Earl De La Warr,
once entertained George III and greatly pleased his Majesty by
arranging that hot rolls from his favourite London baker should
be brought to the house each day wrapped in hot flannel and
born by relays of horsemen. They valued the right things in
those days.

Past Aston Ferry we reach HAMBLEDEN LOCK with its long
weir and lasher and its white weather-boarded mill, which still
grinds corn, though no longer with water power. The group of
buildings here is called MILL END and the Chiltern village of
HAMBLEDEN itself lies a mile to the north. It is worth a visit,
because not only is it a pretty village in itself with its cottages
and church placed round a triangular green, but inside the
church are several good monuments. The best is the d'Oyley
tomb, one of the finest Caroline alabaster monuments to be
seen anywhere in England. It contains the kneeling effigies of
Sir Cope d'Oyley, 'who put on immortality, 1633' and of his
wife and ten children, the artist-craftsman being almost certainly John Hargrave, a London mason. Lady d'Oyley, by the way,
was sister of Francis Quarles, poet laureate to King James.

In the village are the remains of a Roman villa built in A.D.
50 and occupied thereafter for three hundred years. Its remains
of tiles, mosaic floors, pottery and writing implements are now
contained in a small museum built here by Lord Hambleden in
1913.

Above Hambleden Lock the landscape becomes more sophisticated and much of it is deliberately planted with decorative
trees. Large houses and some cottages line the bank on the
right, and behind them the Cotswold landscape stretches away
to distant beechwoods. One of the houses is GREENLANDS built
originally in 1604 when it became the seat of the d'Oyleys, but
it was enlarged and converted in 1853 into a dull Italianate
mansion. Then it was acquired by W. H. Smith, son of the
founder of the famous booksellers, and it was recently presented
by Lord Hambleden to the nation as an Administrative Staff
College.

Just above Greenlands is Regatta, or TEMPLE, ISLAND with
its classical temple, really a cottage, a piece of landscape decoration typical of the 18th century. Mrs. Lybbe-Powys in her

diary tells us that this charming decoration was built for Mr. Freeman of Fawley Court and was designed by James Wyatt. That was in 1771 when Wyatt was young and before he became Surveyor-General and a great man. The Temple looks down the famous regatta reach, where, if the regatta season is on, white-painted booms and posts will have been erected right down to Henley, whose picturesque cluster of bridge, church and houses can be seen closing the river perspective a mile away.

A short distance along on the left is the tiny village of REMENHAM with a small church which we need not visit. In its churchyard lies buried Caleb Gould, once a lock-keeper at Hambleden, who died in 1836. He seems to have been a renowned local figure who dressed in a long coat with many buttons and sold to bargemen and others bread which he baked in a large oven behind his cottage. He is also known to have consumed a plate of onion porridge every night for his supper, and, since he lived to be 92, he may have a rule of good health to teach us.

Opposite Remenham, now unaccountably screened from the river by a belt of trees, lies FAWLEY COURT built by Christopher Wren in the 1680s but having Victorian additions. Its estate was a No Man's Land during the Civil War when Cromwell held Henley. Both the original Fawley Court and Greenlands were then badly knocked about. Greenlands, held by the Royalists, withstood a siege of six months, at the end of which it was almost in ruins. Evidence of the bombardment it sustained was provided during its enlargement in the 19th century when a large crop of cannon-balls was unearthed in the grounds. Bulstrode Whitelock, owner of Fawley Court at that time, has left a pathetic record of the wanton destruction of his property caused by the Cavaliers who 'did all the mischief and spoil that malice and enmity could provoke barbarian mercenaries to commit.' Clearly not all the waste and destruction of that uneasy period were caused by the Roundheads.

HENLEY is a very old town, the name meaning literally in Saxon the Old Place, but its present character is largely Georgian. Though at one time a bustling coaching stage on the Oxford run, it now comes alive only once a year during the Regatta (aptly termed the Goodwood of the River), which originated in 1829 at the same time as the University Boat Race,

when the Oxford and Cambridge crews met for the first time
on the Henley Mile. The Regatta did not get into its stride,
however, until 1839 when the eight of Trinity College, Cambridge, won the Grand Challenge Cup. Thereafter it continued
to grow in popularity, thanks partly to the encouragement of
the Prince Consort, who turned it into a royal event.

The stone bridge with its balustrade and five arches is one
of the most graceful on the Thames. It was built in 1787 to a
design by a Mr. Hayward who died before the bridge was
built; he has a monument in the near-by church. On the key-
stones on each side of the centre arch are carved the masks of
Thames (see title-page) and Isis, the work of the Hon. Mrs.
Damer, a talented sculptress, whose father, General Conway,
once owned the great house and grounds of Park Place which
lies about a mile up river. She was also the cousin of Horace
Walpole who left her his house at Strawberry Hill for life.

Close to the bridge is the church, a genuine late Gothic
building with a fine post-Reformation tower. It is otherwise
not of great interest, though its Chantry House of about 1400
is worth inspecting. In the churchyard lies Richard Jennings,
master-carpenter of St. Paul's Cathedral, whose father was a
Henley bargemaster, while along the west of the churchyard is
a row of Gothic almshouses in white stucco, lettered at the
southern end: 'Endowed by John Longland, Bishop of Lincoln,
1547. Rebuilt 1830'. The south end of the row adjoins a
splendid example of an early Georgian brick house which
faces Hart Street. Look, now, from across the street at the whole
complex here—the west end of the church with the tower, the
pavement raised above the road and protected by a curve of
iron railings, the ornate Victorian fountain backed by the
churchyard, the charming row of white almshouses of 1830.
and next to that the dignified façade of sash windows and red
and yellow brick of the Georgian house. The picture is curiously
pleasing though it is as a whole quite unplanned and unpremeditated—a typical English country town scene which
should surely teach our modern perfectionist architects that
townscape is less a matter of producing buildings that are in-
dividually good than of building to create harmonious pictures
in the streets wherever you look. This is something extremely
difficult to achieve consciously and requires a very subtle,

sensitive imagination which is able to turn the limitations of space *and time as well* into creative advantages.

A stroll round the town is recommended in order to discover other street pictures of this kind and also a number of pleasant old houses and inns in the streets. The stroll should take in the famous Fair Mile, the dramatic avenue approach to the town from the west.

MARSH LOCK lies about a mile above Henley. Its cottage has the wise and kindly look of a simple old countryman, the garden is one of those which win prizes and the whole landscape here is most agreeable—partly on account of the trees, partly on account of the towpath which swings right out into the river on a long timber bridge, runs between the lock and the weir and then sweeps in a wide curve back to land again.

The Rev. Humphrey Gainsborough, brother of the great painter and minister at Henley Congregational Church, had something to do with the building of the original pound lock here in 1773. He seems to have been a man of parts with a gift for engineering, who counted James Watt among his friends. He was the builder of the archway we shall find a short way up.

Beyond the lock you can just see the top of the great house of PARK PLACE above the trees on the Berkshire side. This is not the original house which stood here but was built in a French Renaissance manner in the 1870s. The grounds, however, were laid out in the 18th century by James 'Athenian' Stuart, architect and landscape gardener. The original house was built for the Duke of Hamilton and was for a time, like Cliveden, the residence of Frederick, Prince of Wales, father of George III. Towards the end of the 18th century a Major Conway obtained it and it was he more than the other owners who developed the grounds. He did so with tremendous zeal especially in providing the garden decorations which Horace Walpole has described in his *Hieroglyphic Tales*. They include an obelisk formed from the original steeple of St. Bride's, Fleet Street, various artificial ruins, a subterranean passage leading to a Roman amphitheatre and a Druids' Temple. This curious temple was discovered in the Isle of Jersey in 1785 when Conway was Governor of the island. It was presented to him when he left and he had it set up in his garden exactly as it had been when found. It consists of large stone slabs about seven feet high set in a circle of sixty-five feet circumference within which rough niches are composed. The so-called temple is in fact a tomb and the niches once contained corpses—probably those of chieftains. Originally a mound of earth covered the whole.

By the waterside stands a Victorian boathouse of character spoiled recently during alterations when the niches containing statues of saints were filled in. At its side a wooded glade known as The Happy Valley ascends into the grounds, framed by Gainsborough's arch which is composed of large, rough, radiating stones taken from the ruins of Reading Abbey and known locally as The Ragged Arches.

Ahead on the left we see the entrance to the long and lovely HENNERTON BACKWATER and then pass by some islands which with their spindly, unhappy-looking trees give the appearance of a tropical swamp. We pass LOWER SHIPLAKE with its wealthy middle-class houses and sweep round an open plain to WARGRAVE, another pretty village with an old, though much restored, church (containing the tomb of Madame Tussaud of the waxworks), two 17th-century inns, a Queen Anne Vicarage and two quaint buildings designed by Cole Adams in 1900 in the Art Nouveau style called Woodclyffe Hall and the Woodclyffe Institute.

Beyond the Wargrave bend an ugly railway bridge crosses the river and then, just below Shiplake Lock, the RIVER LODDEN flows into the Thames. About three-quarters of a mile up, this tributary is linked to the Thames by the St. Patrick's Stream and it is said that one can dodge the lock in a small boat by working against the strong current of the Lodden and then turning off onto this backwater. Here a warning should be given against a certain characteristic of the Lodden which is curious and hard to explain. Those who swim *against* its current are invariably afflicted afterwards by vomiting. No one will believe this who has not experimented, but the result is always the same.

We will moor for a while on the right just above SHIPLAKE LOCK, because not only is it one of the prettiest mooring spots on the river but we shall be able to take an enjoyable walk from here to Shiplake Church along a bridle path which runs along the side of a hill for about a mile parallel to the river. As we set off we notice on the lock island opposite a row of willows and

Shiplake Church

behind them some large white tents, which can be hired from the Thames Conservancy for holidays. The lock itself is unremarkable but has another good example of those timber footbridges. SHIPLAKE CHURCH is worth inspecting on account of its unusual stained glass windows of brilliant colouring and curious bold designs which were made in France in the 15th century. In the 19th century they were bought from the monks of St. Bertin Abbey, St. Omer, where they had lain buried since the French Revolution. Lord Tennyson was married in this church.

In just over two miles we reach SONNING with its beautiful 17th-century bridge of mellowed brick. The village is one of the prettiest and best preserved on the river—old, harmonious, picturesque and rich with the colours and textures of weathered materials—'an upland town', as Leland describes it, 'set on fair and commodious ground, beneath which the Tamise runneth in a pleasant vale', or to use the modern, more sentimental phrase of Jerome K. Jerome, 'the most fairy-like little nook on the River'. The best description of the place, however, comes in *Murray's Berkshire Guide*: 'White and cream-walled and brick houses decorated with roses, honeysuckle, jasmine and clematis, carefully trained to climb over the corners of some of the old

tiled roofs, line the streets of this rich river resort which is un-
disturbed by a main road and tinged (even on a grey day out
of season) with an Edwardian Holiday, or musical-comedy,
gaiety . . . In the short village streets are many 17th- and 18th-
century houses, or parts of houses . . . judiciously altered according to an agreeable kind of small, collective, Edwardian feeling
for picturesque comfort.' A slight hilliness in the place adds to
the interest of the street pictures, especially to that seen from
the east corner of the Deanery Garden where an ancient brick
wall runs down the edge of the street to an early cast-iron pump
and a group of cottages—a wall which surrounded a palace for
the Bishops of Salisbury up to the 16th century and now en-
compasses a house and garden built in 1900 for the founder of
the *Country Life* magazine by Sir Edwin Lutyens. This is an
early country house of his which approaches a work of genius.
Sonning Church, standing near the river, has a famous peal of
bells and a few interesting monuments, notably the Rich Monument of 1667 under the tower consisting of four cherubs supporting a black marble slab on which stand two large carved
white urns.

Past a white boarded mill below which the mill stream water
comes foaming, and then along a tree-shrouded stretch we
reach SONNING LOCK, the highest upstream of the first eight
locks built under the 1770 Act. It is famed for its garden,
which under the reign of Mr. Edward Light held the challenge
cup for the best-kept lock and garden for 13 years. His successor,
Mr. Prince, is also a gardening enthusiast and seems likely to
follow the tradition. It is to be hoped, however, that he will
break some of the regimented formality of the beds along the
lock sides which have less attraction than the informal terraces
below the lock. Apart from its garden, Sonning Lock is renowned for the colourful characters of its keepers—another
tradition which Mr. Prince seems likely to maintain, for standing at the paddle wheels of his lock gates in white shirt sleeves
and white peaked cap he is an imposing figure who radiates
the authority of an admiral on the bridge of his flag ship.

A former keeper appointed in 1845 named John Sadler
achieved recognition both as a bee-keeper and a minor poet,
and was parish clerk at Sonning for 33 years. He became
famous as an apiarist and invented the Berkshire hive. His

verses dealt mainly with the river and with his hobby, the best being his naïve, didactic eclogue entitled *Special Pleas for Honey Bees*. Part of it runs:

> They nothing care for vaulted dome, but keep it cool and give them room.
> Though to the south their house be made, by all means keep it in the shade;
> For when the weather cold becomes, they cluster well beneath the combs;
> But if they get intensely warm, nothing is left them but to swarm . . .
> I think enough is said to show bees are the pets you ought to know.
> They give you pleasure, bring you gain; with but the smallest risk of pain.
> Long has it proverbial been that industry in bees is seen:
> This lesson then for me and you: Work while there is work to do.

From Sonning up to the lock and beyond, the towpath runs beneath the overhanging trees of Holme Park on the Berkshire bank and is called locally The Thames Parade. Then suddenly the river magic is shattered. Ahead a great power station rears up from a vacant flat of waste land—a clear case for screening by trees. Now we are in for nearly three miles of squalor, at least on the Berkshire side—the gas works, railway sidings, unfeeling walls of grimy machine-made bricks, rusting corrugated iron roofs, chaos of overhead wires all set amidst tufts of sooty, half-dead grass while in the distance rise the factory chimneys above the grey slate roofs of READING, that ancient town ' 'mong other things so widely known for biscuits, seeds and sauce.' This is anti-Thames.

> At Reading once arrived, clear Kennet overtakes
> Her lord, the stately Thames; which that great flood again,
> With many signes of joy, doth kindly entertain.

So sang Drayton. Now the signs of joy as we pass the dismal entrance to the Kennet and Avon Navigation are not evident. Close your eyes then as we drift past these obtrusions and listen instead to a brief description of the Berkshire capital, which has become, next to London, the largest town in the Valley.

Since the site between the Kennet and the Thames formed a good natural stronghold, Reading has been a settlement since early times, though it did not become important until in 1121 Henry I founded an abbey here which grew into one of the four

great abbeys of the south (the others being Glastonbury, Abingdon and St. Albans). It flourished until 1539 when the last
Abbot, Hugh Faringdon, resisting the Defender of the Faith,
was hanged, drawn and quartered with two of his monks outside the abbey entrance. Like many of its kind the abbey was
then converted into a palace. Charles I was the last to occupy
it and, after being battered by Parliamentary cannon balls in
the Civil War, it became a quarry. A few of its stones still stand
in the Forbury Gardens which now occupy the former 'Fau-
bourg', or outer court, of the palace.

Though never of great strategic importance, the town has seen
some fighting. The Danes and Saxons struggled here in 870;
then it was burned down by the Danes in 1006; during the
Civil War it was occupied in turn by both sides and during the
almost bloodless revolution of 1688, a street battle was fought
here between the supporters of William of Orange and some
Irish mercenaries of James II. After the Reformation the town
seems to have become a fairly important centre of distribution,
especially for cloth and wool, and Defoe describes it as 'A very
large and wealthy Town, handsomely built, the Inhabitants
rich, and driving a very great Trade'. Though it is no longer
on the whole handsomely built, Reading still drives a very great
trade and it is worth a visit, for it is less depressing within than
it appears to be from the river.

Of great interest is the fascinating museum of finds from the
near-by town of Silchester, displaying, with models and drawings, the life, buildings and planning of a flourishing Romano-
British city. Of the four churches, two are notable—the cathedral church of St. Mary's which was virtually rebuilt in the
1550s with materials taken from the Abbey, and Greyfriars'
Church in Friar Street which has a good west window. Its
parsonage is a good classic design by Sir John Soane (1753-
1837) who was also responsible for the obelisk in Market Place.
(Soane, incidentally was born beside the Thames, though
higher up at Whitchurch. He is, of course, best known for his
work at the Bank of England). Reading also possesses a number
of pleasant Georgian houses and a few also of the 17th century
which stand in Castle Street. Note also a small bridge of dis-
tinction across the Kennet called High Bridge which was built
in 1788.

Across the river on the Oxfordshire side (we have been on
the edge of Oxfordshire since half-way up the Henley Reach),
lies CAVERSHAM—a suburb of Reading and mostly a scatter-
ing of soulless modern villas dominated in the distance by the
disdainful mansion of Caversham Park House which was rebuilt in 1854.

As the water fills Caversham Lock this part of our journey
may well conclude with an anecdote of the district which reveals something of the hearty, humorous, bullying character
of Henry VIII and may also increase your appetite for lunch.
It has been recorded by Fuller in his *Church History* in the vivid
and robust style of his period. Describing it as a pleasant and
true story, he relates:

King Henry VIII as he was hunting in Windsor Forest, either casually lost, or
(more probably) wilfully losing himself, struck down about dinner-time to the
Abbey of Reading, when disguising himself, much for delight (more for discovery
to see unseen) he was invited to the Abbot's table, and passed for one of the King's
guards, a place to which the proportion of his person might properly entitle him.
A sirloin of beef was set before him (so knighted, saith tradition, by this King
Henry) on which the King laid on lustily, not disgracing one of that place, for
whom he was mistaken. Well fare thy heart (quoth the Abbot) and here in a cup
of sack I remember the health of his Grace your Master; I would give an hundred
pounds on the condition I could feed so heartily on beef as you do. Alas! my weak
and squeasie stomach will hardly digest the wing of a small rabbet or chicken.
The King pleasantly pledged him, and heartily thanked him for his good chear;
after dinner departed, as undiscovered as he came thither. Some weeks after, the
Abbot was sent for by a Pursuivant, brought up to London, clapt in the Tower,
kept close prisoner, fed for a short time on bread and water; yet not so empty his
body of food, as his mind was filled with fears, creating many suspitions to himself,
when, and how he had incurred the King's displeasure. At last a sirloin of beef
was set before him, on which the Abbot fed as the farmer of his grange, and verified
the proverb, that two hungry meals make the third a glutton. In springs King
Henry, out of a private lobbie, where he had placed himself the invisible spectator
of the Abbot's behaviour; My Lord (quoth the King) presently deposit your
hundred pounds in gold, or else no going hence all the daies of your life. I have
been your physician, to cure you of your squeazie stomach; and here, as I deserve,
I demand my fee for the same. The Abbot down with his dust, and glad he had
escaped so, returning to Reading, as somewhat lighter in purse, so much more
merrier in heart than when he came thence.

6

Looking Forward

ONCE PAST READING'S TWO MODERN concrete road bridges
the scene greatly improves. A long strip of municipal park
runs along on the left for about a mile, while on the right
the bank slopes up a low hill covered with trees, which make
room here and there for some fretted, turreted Edwardian
dwellings. Then a tentacle of Reading obtrudes again until at
TILEHURST a railway station stands high up above a great
brick retaining wall right on the riverside, not without a
certain effect of accidental drama. There follows an outcrop of
bungalows behind which lies PURLEY PARK, whose grounds
have been divided in two by the railway line. The house is a
large, plain classic structure built in 1795 by Wyatt. Near it
stands a more interesting house called PURLEY HALL built of
brick and stone early in the 17th century and altered a century
later. Here Warren Hastings resided while awaiting his trial.

Beyond MAPLEDURHAM LOCK the river has entirely re-
covered from her brief nervous breakdown. Her lost serenity
returns and, by contrast, seems the sweeter. Let us now tie up
in the millstream above the lock on the Oxfordshire side to
brew a cup of tea before inspecting Mapledurham village.
With the whiff of burning methylated spirits in your nose and
the hiss of the primus stove in your ears, invoking memories of
brief holiday escapes to freedom, the open air and zestful good
health, permit the author to digress for a chapter on the possible
future of the Thames—on how we can preserve her ageless
youth and beauty for ourselves and posterity.

The broad argument is that this Stream of Pleasure can only
be preserved as such if it becomes established as a National
Park under the National Parks and Access to the Countryside
Act of 1949.

But what is a National Park? It is not a park in the usual, formal sense at all and has been officially defined as:

An extensive area of beautiful and relatively wild country in which, for the nation's benefit and by appropriate national decision and action, (a) the characteristic landscape beauty is strictly preserved (b) access and facilities for public open-air enjoyment are amply provided (c) the wild life and buildings and places of architectural and historic interest are suitably protected, while (d) established farming use is effectively maintained.

Already the National Parks Commission, which was set up after the Act was passed, has designated six areas as National Parkland—Snowdonia, the Lakes, the Peak District, Dartmoor, the Pembrokeshire Coast, and the North Yorkshire Moors. The suggestion made here is that the Thames above Teddington should be the next on the list—for the following reasons.

The Thames is the one great natural feature of the Greater London Region; and that part of it lying to the west of the Wen, especially that above Teddington Lock where the Thames Conservancy takes over from the Port of London Authority, satisfactorily combines the two functions of supplying London with water and of acting as a recreational strip. It is, and has been for a century, a public pleasure park in fact if not in name, and relatively little is now required in legislation, planning and cost to convert the river into a complete park both in fact and in name, and *to preserve it as such*.

The Thames provides a pleasure resort not only for Londoners but for all who live in the thickly populated area of Southern England, including those towns which lie on or near its banks such as Slough, Windsor, Reading, Oxford and Swindon. Moreover the river is not just a regional amenity; it is a national possession—virtually an open-air museum of English culture, containing the history and monuments of centuries.

As we have seen, there has always been conflict between the various users of the river, formerly between boaters, millers and fishermen, more recently between the general public and owners of riparian property. This latter conflict reached a peak during the last century and the result was that a Select Committee was set up in 1884 to 'enquire into the operation of the Acts for the Preservation of the Thames and the steps which are necessary to secure the enjoyment of the River as a place of Recreation'. What the Committee did definitely establish was that though fishing rights above Staines might be private, 'the rights of the public to move boats over any and every part of the river through which Thames water flows, as an ancient and free highway, wherever they are not of necessity and, for the time, excluded by the requirements of the navigation, should be clearly declared.' The river itself is thus by ancient right a public place and as the spinal cord of a National Linear Park it presents no legal complications.

The legal position of the towpath as a public right of way is more complex and will need clearing up. The difficulties, however, are easy to overcome with the powers now available, and the new powers provided by the National Parks Act would allow the State provision of improvements and amenities for recreation on the Thames as a whole, once it had been designated as a National Park. If the river is to become such a park, all these powers may have to be used and private owners of riparian land will be required to co-operate. Things will go much more smoothly if this co-operation is willing and constructive, and it should be made clear to private owners by the authorities that if they have to make some immediate sacrifices everyone, including themselves, will benefit in the long run and their private battles to preserve the beauties of the river they love will have been won for them once and for all.

Most of the Thames has retained its charm of isolation and in the 135 miles between Teddington and Cricklade there is great variety of scene within the typical character. There are already signs, however, of conflict of uses, and of the failure to make the right kind of provisions for the various users. The status of a National Park could put these things right.

Mere chance is mainly responsible for the preservation of the river character up to the present time—decline of water transport as competition developed with rail and road, the fertility and dampness of the alluvial soil producing rich vegetation, the curtailment of building by the war, the existence of wide tracts of floodland tending to preclude too much building by the river, the careful maintenance of riverside parks and gardens by their proud owners. Perhaps, too, the general attitude among all classes towards the river as a result of its traditional use for pleasure and recreation has produced an unconscious recognition of a River Culture which may have acted as a subtle, sensitising force on the landscape.

But it is too dangerous to leave the landscape to the whims of chance any longer, even under existing planning controls, which are still largely negative ones. A dynamic, creative approach is needed to preserve and improve one of the most accessible, one of the most interesting and beautiful of large-scale public pleasure parks in England—and the most unusual. It is relatively unspoiled, it is picturesque, it can be enjoyed according to temperament either in crowded places or in remote retreat, it offers many facilities for sport and recreation in delightful surroundings at a time when leisure for all has come to stay and will steadily grow as mechanisation of industry increases. It offers boating, walking, fishing and all the pastimes associated with these activities—sunbathing, camping, exploration and the study of nature, archaeology, history, architecture, sketching and painting, reading, talking, picknicking, dreaming, junketting, lovemaking—and all beside the soul's ease, the soothing, symbolic, inexhaustible stream.

The proposal to establish a Riverside Walk along the towpath from Teddington to Cricklade has already been officially proposed and seems likely to be put into effect. But is this enough? The idea that this walk should be considered as part of a larger whole—the Thames Linear Park—has not yet been publicly mooted. The Walk must, of course, be a basic element in such a park and would act as its necessary backbone, but much more than that is needed. The spinal cord in the form of the river itself and the flesh to clothe the whole—the trees and planting, the right kinds of buildings, the proper amenities, the establishment of reservations in certain beauty spots and so on—cannot be disregarded if the Walk is to have any value.

The idea of a continuous riverside walk is not a new one. The Thames River Preservation Committee of 1884 expressed the view that such a walk was desirable and recorded that a similar idea had been put forward in 1793. Now, largely through the initiative of the Thames Conservancy Board, the scheme is almost certain to go through. The idea is that the walk should run from the tidal limit at Teddington, Middlesex, to Cricklade, Gloucestershire, which is practically at the source of the river.

I

(The only comparable long-distance foot route is the Pennine Way). The Walk would follow, as closely as possible, the existing towpath, much of which is in fact, if not in law, now open to the public, the worst break occurring at the royal Home Park opposite Datchet, which is at present closed off except to (non-existent) bargees and their horses. A completely new walk would have to be constructed from Inglesham, where the tow-path now ends, up to Cricklade, but as this would run along meadowland most of the way, this should not present many difficulties. A good deal of work is needed to repair erosion and crumbling of the banks and according to a survey made in 1948 nearly 13,000 feet of towpath at 42 points need protective work. The Board has asked that a 25 feet wide strip of land should be set aside as a public open space along the towpath to prevent development which might interfere with the walk. Where the towpath, so to speak, crosses the river, either ferries will be organised or foot bridges will be built, but, wherever possible, crossings will be made at locks. The cost has been estimated at £50,000 a year for several years and after that a much lower upkeep cost. It is hoped that the National Parks Commission, in other words the Nation, will pay the bulk of the cost and that the other authorities concerned, such as local councils, will each pay merely a token share.

That, then, is the position of the Towpath Scheme at the time of writing. The Thames Linear Park is therefore already half-way to realization, because the path is the core of such a park, its *sine qua non*. The path articulates and establishes its unique linear quality. It also establishes its character as a *park*, in that a park is a place of ease and refreshment artificially land-scaped with trees, plants and structures, and, above all, with water, one of the most valuable materials of the landscape de-signer. The river in the Thames Line can thus be considered in a sense as an appendage to the towpath, a kind of ornamental lake on which one can, of course, disport oneself, but which is fundamentally a decorative feature to be seen from the land. And it must be *continuous*. This is an important psychological point, a matter of feeling. Its importance can easily be grasped if one considers the towpath as being broken and discontinuous as it is at present, for then the linear quality of the park is at once destroyed.

To one's atavistic being, communication, travel and exploration are best carried out on foot, otherwise sensations of difficulty and thoughts of worrying barriers to be overcome arise. Water to one's subconscious mind is a barrier and not the first choice as a means of mobility—a dug-out must be built, unknown hazards must be faced, one's arms are not free for defence or for food-gathering or eating. On the other hand, the forest track is familiar and there life is better understood and more easily controlled. The towpath can be considered as a native bush track, more natural, safer and easier (and incidentally, cheaper) than the river as a line of travel.

Its variety makes it so agreeable a walk, and what it lacks in hilliness is amply repaid by the landscape effects provided by the water and by the rapid contrast of scene. Surprises are continual as the track winds from one decorative, built-up clearing to another between seemingly natural country. It waves along the side of the river, across the river and even occasionally, as at Marsh Lock, along and above the river. It sometimes undulates over bridges, but mostly it goes on its horizontal way, splitting in two at lock rollers so that a part descends to the level of the water below; pausing for a moment at a lock, where, as at Boulter's, it may, so to speak, sit down for a moment and spread its legs; wandering off round a lock island to stride a weir; narrowing along a grassy, bucolic reach as at Shifford, or widening out to gravel when it reaches a populated area as at Molesey; occasionally wandering away from the river for a short while as at Marlow, where it joins a road, passes some Regency houses and then runs down a twitton to emerge to a sight of the river again at the end of a lane. Obstacles on the line provide breaks, add to its variety, articulate and contain its direction by means of such things as white gates between meadows—as above Shiplake Lock or at Basildon.

The river itself is fed by streams but the towpath also has its tributaries—tracks, lanes and bridle paths that wind down the valley slopes and so link the towpath with the whole national system of footpaths. Up these a temporary break from the level walk can be made and grand views of the countryside obtained as at Sinodun Hill and Streatley.

What, now, of the Line as a whole—the towpath-plus-river? Before we can preserve and refurbish it in its established style, we must understand quite clearly the constituents of that style and character. We must analyse it. It consists of three elements: first, its winding, linear form which makes the Thames a unique kind of park; secondly, its sense of remoteness and escape from the outer world, whether screened by foliage or opened out to broad landscape; thirdly, its sudden, swift surprises, its exciting sense of something round the corner, its rapid contrasts as between informal, verdant rusticity and gay, decorative urbanity, both of which possess qualities peculiar to the Thames alone.

The line has an atmosphere of isolation, secrecy and escape which survives even where it passes through a town or winds past some modern intrusion well screened by foliage. Mile after mile of exploration and adventure either afloat or on foot is possible in a world on its own within a world. The route is fixed and immutable and this soothes the mind—soothes but never bores for there is surprise and change at every bend. The river calms us but at the same time stimulates us with an agreeable sense of adventure, and, as we move along in an even, leisurely way, the outside world flows past. Picture follows picture, each a vivid contrast to the next. The height of the bank varies, houses crowd in, overhang and then suddenly stop, leaving us exposed and tiny in a wide panorama. Ramps slide up and fall away. We pass under a bridge and suddenly there is a change of scale from open landscape to a cool, vaulted room.

For example, to take a well-known section: At Maidenhead life is urban, lively, affluent, the outside world of cars and buses obtrudes, but only for an instant. Here the river is wide and busy and a motor road accompanies the river even beyond Boulter's Lock. Then comes the sharp contrast of a narrow, intimate, tree-lined cutting which suddenly opens out to the splendours of Cliveden Reach. On the right a great forested escarpment rises up, and on the left flat, unsullied meadows stretch away to a horizon of trees. Ahead lies a cluster of floating, Turneresque islands and far off above them stands the dramatic block of Cliveden itself, pretentious and uninspired as a building maybe, but of great value as a focus in that landscape. Then the sudden bend into the narrow, friendly approach to Cookham Lock, while the river continues up the weir stream through a superb, informal treescape where the mass of variegated 'bushytops' forms a foil to the powerful banners of the poplars. Beyond Cookham with its low iron bridge comes the sudden change to flat, open country reaching away to the left towards Quarry Woods, while to the right mature Edwardian gardens line the bank to Bourne End.

And so on and on, urbanity following wilderness, close intimacy following the view to the horizon with exciting and startling rapidity.

The art of development of the line will consist in preserving this sense of isolation and of rapid change. This involves a peculiar technique. The line must be screened from the outside world and the outside world must be screened from it. Factories and ribbon developement may be near but will be hidden by trees. The reverse, too, will hold good, for where the scene opens out to encompass the surrounding countryside of copse, hills and fields, any boundaries must be concealed—an ugly fence, for example, which may easily ruin a three-mile view, should be replaced by a ha-ha (a sunken barrier) or its equivalent. Thus even where the view is wide, it will be in a sense 'enclosed' as part of the park.

On account both of its innate character, which has been created through the centuries and also on account of its narrow width, the landscape is—and must continue to be—*artificial*. The question to be answered before refurbishing the Line is therefore: What kind of artificiality do we want?

We want, broadly speaking, to create two sorts of interdependent artificiality which act as foils to each other but which are both peculiar to the Thames and form part of its fundamental pattern. Only in this way can the desired sense of isolation (apart from certain established exceptions), the sense of a country on its own, be retained. We want on the one hand to create a wilderness, an apparently natural phenomenon, a kind of miniature Amazon, in the heart of England in order to form the most striking contrast possible with the outer world. We want, on the other hand, where building is dominant, not to conceal the building, if it is of the right kind, but to retain and develop the characteristic Thames style of building.

The first is a matter mainly of planting. The landscape must open out only where the prospect pleases and even where pictures of the outside world intrude they must be made to look like part of your special landscape. Whatever buildings occur in such cases they, too, must form part of this special landscape, or else be concealed.

The second is a matter essentially of special style and special ornament—of special detailing and planting. Wherever the picture is disrupted you can either hide the trouble or you can accept it and turn it to advantage by applying a technique of ornamentation.

By the twin techniques—the sudden transition from Amazonian wilderness to formal ornamentation which often occurs even within one reach, and the acceptance of, and development of, the established character of ornamentation—the peculiar character of the river can be preserved and developed. The transition is swift and sudden; no gentle half-way introductions are needed or desirable. The wavy nature of the Line itself with its closed vistas, punctuated by flagpole, lombardy, pavilion or church spire, helps to create this element of sudden change and surprise. This effect should not be softened but rather emphasised to be as thrilling as the flash of fireworks during Henley Week—suspense, shock, climax.

But what exactly is meant by the special ornamentation? Briefly and suggestively it means bright paintwork with white predominating, the multiplicity of open-air rooms in the form of balconies and verandahs, brilliantly coloured awnings and umbrellas over well-mown lawns, queer little gabled, fretwork boathouses, special kinds of riverside garden plantation, particularly of trees that bloom, the gay, relaxed jungle holiday bungalows where the bush track emerges from the trees into a clearing—those lively, spontaneous, fantastic, harmonious but variegated retreats of leisure. The ornamentation is characterised, too, by its size and scale which is always at a homely, human level and in the so-called 'trim' of river furniture, white fences, simple verges and campshedding of concrete or tarred timber, the Thames Conservancy vernacular of bold wooden mooring posts, locks and bridges. Then there is the formal municipal riverside park in its best form, and such incidents as the white flag pole doubled by its reflection in the still water ahead. The moored boats, also, with their moving reflections will form decorative elements—the slim, white launches with their wicker chairs, the rows of low punts held by their vertical poles, the satisfying forms of the traditional river skiffs and

randans with their seat backs of wrought-iron curlicues, their
pipe-clayed fend-offs and red plush cushions, among all of
which the swans of Her Majesty drift in their serene, protected
arrogance.

So much for the aesthetic principles which should govern the
Thames Linear Park. But what about the practical side of
things? How should one set about organising its creation and
what exactly should be done? Here are some suggestions.

First, a special body should be set up under the National
Parks Commission, composed of representatives of all the interests concerned—Borough, County and Joint Planning Authori-
ties, Thames Conservancy Board, Ministry of Housing and
Local Government, Council for the Preservation of Rural England, Commons, Open Spaces and Footpaths Preservation
Society, Ramblers' Association, Youth Hostels Association,
Anglers' Co-operative Association, Society for the Preservation
of Ancient Buildings, the Georgian Group, the Royal Fine Art
Commission, the various water boards, riparian owners' association, boat owners' association and so on. Let us call it the
Thames National Park Joint Board. Working for that council
should be a full-time executive staff capable of a creative realization of the Park.

Before attacking any job you must know two things clearly.
First, what it is you want. Secondly, what are the existing conditions from which you have to start.

The first, the objective, which the Joint Board should have
before it, is now clear enough. It is to preserve the Thames
River and its immediate environs from Teddington to Cricklade
as a National Linear Park; to develop and enhance its distinctive

visual character; to improve all its facilities for recreation; to reconcile conflicting interests of users (as, for example, between the seeker of solitude and the gregarious, as between farmer and camper, as between angler and boater); in particular to develop and maintain the towpath as an uninterrupted pedestrian way as the core of the Line.

The second, the discovery of existing conditions, can be accomplished by carrying out a thorough survey to find out:

(1) The extent to which the river is now used for various purposes—economic, cultural, recreational.

(2) The extent to which the river could be used as a National Park for these purposes without being overloaded and so spoiling the very character which is to be preserved.

(3) The extent to which present amenities fall short of requirements in such matters as boating stations (now among the most unsightly of riverside structures), public landing stages in towns and villages (now quite inadequate), refreshment facilities, hostels and hotels, camping sites (whether for single tents or many), moorings and winter storage for private boats (now very overcrowded; here co-operation with the Wey River and Basingstoke Canal should be considered), public facilities at locks such as drinking water supply and refuse dumps, fishing reserves and stocking.

(4) Where, and to what extent, the landscape is now blighted by factories, poor housing, railway bridges, shacks and so on. (Hurley Village, for example, though at one of the loveliest parts of the river, is unkempt and marred by a chaotic caravan town; the approach to Abingdon is spoiled by callow municipal housing and some unsightly monuments to electrical engineering).

(5) What areas should be scheduled as reservations? (The 1929 Survey of the Thames Valley by the Council for the Preservation of Rural England lists the following twenty:—Beacon Hill, Wytham Hill and Park, Bagley Wood, Nuneham Courtenay, Andersey Island, Culham and Sutton Courtenay Flats, Long Wittenham Flats, Dorchester Levels, Sinodun Hill, Wallingford (including the flats on the Oxfordshire bank), the Goring Gap, Sonning Village and environs, Henley and environs, Hambleden and Mill End, Hurley Reach, Quarry Woods, Cliveden Woods, Home Park at Windsor, Eton playing fields and adjacent areas, Cooper's Hill. To that list the author would add Abingdon and Marlow).

(6) What built-up areas should be scheduled for clearance as open space? (These mostly lie below Staines though there are floodlands above at several points now built over which should be cleared).

(7) What is the condition of existing 'trim', both in its physical state and in its design qualities, e.g. towpath gates, river posts, verges, embanking, landing stages?

(8) What parts of the river are suitable for special purposes, e.g. below Cricklade, at Radcot, New Bridge and Little Wittenham for fishing; Dorchester and Streatley for country walking; Bourne End, Godstow and Culham for sailing; Abingdon and Bray for good food; Shifford Cut for contemplative retirement, and so on?

(9) What are the special needs of the towpath as a continuous walk—legal

embanking, campshedding (facing of piles and boarding to resist water action on a bank, i.e. sheathing the *champ*), ferries, footbridges, camp sites, youth hostels, junctions with local footpaths and so with the whole national footpath system, eyesores to be removed or mitigated? (A good deal of this planning work has already been done by the Thames Conservancy).

(10) What ancient monuments on or near the Line should be preserved and maintained—bridges, churches, houses, mills, villages?

(11) What are the typical flora and fauna of the river and how can they be preserved and protected?

(12) What are the conditions of the islands and eyots?

(13) What are the possibilities of extending the park to include the Basingstoke Canal, the Oxford Canal, the Kennet and Avon Navigation, and the now derelict Thames and Severn Canal?

Then comes the plan of work to be accomplished. Planning as a whole should be imaginative, subtle and, above all, unobtrusive in order to avoid that inhuman, death-dealing sense of official power. The following points are worth considering:

(1) Scheme of tree planting to be instituted immediately, especially where screening is desirable. Characteristic informality and types of trees to be retained.

(2) The continuous Riverside Walk from Teddington to Cricklade to be completed at first opportunity.

(3) Construction of new amenity buildings—such as hostels, cafés, boating stations, etc.

(4) Construction of new mooring basins for private boats. The use of disused gravel pits should be considered in this connection for they need not form landscape scars, but if properly planted and tended could make pleasing ornamental lakes. The pits near Wraysbury provide an example.

(5) Construction of new landing stages and temporary moorings at towns and villages. These are now inadequate and where they do exist, as on the Berkshire side above Maidenhead Bridge, are gross in design and of use only to boats of very shallow draft. The main cause of this inadequacy is not merely lack of initiative of local councils, but the lack of a public mooring tradition on the upper river. The public has never owned the right to land anywhere above Staines.

(6) Steps to be taken to preserve open spaces, towns and villages scheduled as reservations.

(7) Eyesores and blight to be removed or ameliorated and areas scheduled for clearance to be cleared as opportunity allows.

(8) All future building along the river to be strictly controlled and all building to be prohibited on floodland.

(9) Plans to be prepared for preserving and enhancing riverside towns *as* riverside towns. The building of a new Water Town at a point somewhere near the half-way point of the Line to be considered, as on the flats below Quarry Woods; such a town to serve as an important river centre, containing riverside homes for those who like living by water, boatyards and the headquarters of river clubs and societies and acting as a focus of the Park. This would form a necessary social

centre for pleasurable river activities such as water carnivals and gay river functions of every sort. (A suggestion for such a town surrounding a lagoon was made
in *The Architectural Review* for July 1950 in the imaginative drawings of Mr. Gordon
Cullen).

(10) Islands and eyots and their vegetation and wild life to be preserved.

(11) Fishing facilities to be increased. There are now two million anglers in
Great Britain and the number is growing. On the Thames the fishing is almost
entirely coarse and to help the coarse fisherman the first aim must be to keep the
river as unpolluted as possible, a task for which the Thames Conservancy is
responsible but in which it is now hampered by inadequate legislative backing.
Areas such as a few of the backwaters might be set aside as fishing reserves. Lagoons
in riverside meadows could be dug, disused gravel pits could be used and tributary
streams now piped or culverted could be opened up to provide water free from
wave wash and the noise from passing boats.

(12) All new electric cables and wires within sight of the river to be laid under
ground, and existing overhead cables to be gradually taken down and laid below
ground. This may be costly but it is essential if the river is not to be ruined by
nightmarish 'wirescapes'.

(13) The water to be increasingly purified, especially of industrial and sewage
effluents. Soil and rubbish dumping into the water from river craft to be firmly
discouraged.

(14) General recommendations to be prepared and published for the guidance
of riverside dwellers and workers on the treatment of boat stations, cafés and
pubs, riverside bungalows and gardens. (Garden owners might be encouraged
by annual competitions among themselves as the lock keepers are at present).
Recommendations, too, might be published for the treatment of landing stages,
verges and general 'trim.'

(15) Facilities for holiday makers to be improved at locks, such as the provision
of easily accessible drinking water, dumps for rubbish, 'comfort stations', and,
perhaps at certain standard distances from locks and recognizable by unobtrusive
standard signs, pits for night soil. (This soil combined with layers of rotting
vegetation would provide gardening lock keepers with the best manure in the
world). A good local map might be provided on the notice board of each lock
showing local footpaths which link up with the towpath, places of historic and
architectural interest in the neighbourhood, local beauty spots, good moorings,
camping sites, bathing spots, nearest shops, post office and railway station,
churches, pubs, hostels and so on.

The threats to the Thames as a pleasure resort are already
too evident in many places. That is why its establishment as an
official National Park is urgently needed and why the author
makes no attempt to excuse himself for having interrupted the
journey to discourse on a subject near to his heart. The matter
is now off his chest, so let us be on our way again.

7

Reading to Oxford

THE MILL, THE CHURCH, THE ALMSHOUSES and the mansion of MAPLEDURHAM have caught the eyes of many generations of painters, good and bad, so rich are they in form, texture, colour and atmosphere. The timber mill with its water-wheel is especially attractive and is one of the oldest existing mills on the river, but unfortunately it has now reached a point of decay that goes beyond even that of melancholy pleasure.

The late-Gothic church with its square tower, chequer-boarded in brick and flint, is interesting in having a private mortuary chapel, railed and curtained off from the body of the established church, for the use of the Roman Catholic family of Blount, who have owned the fine house here since it was first built in 1581 by Sir Michael Blount, Lieutenant of the Tower of London. The interior of the church itself has a painted ceiling, a good old font and a sad, sweet smell of varnished pine.

MAPLEDURHAM HOUSE (meaning the house among the maple trees) is acclaimed by many as one of the finest Tudor houses in England. Certainly the approach from the east down the mile long avenue of stately elms is grand—an avenue to which the legend is attached that when a Blount dies, one of the elms comes crashing down. The house is typical of the period just before the Gothic manner was superseded in a revolutionary way by the classical ideas imported from Renaissance Italy, for it has patterned brickwork, fretted, decorated chimneys, gables, symmetrical plan shaped like an E and tall rooms lit by great mullioned and transomed windows. Inside the house, it is rumoured, are a number of secret rooms and passages used during the Civil War by the Royalists for the hiding of soldiers, and earlier for the hiding of priests.

In the wall on the east of the churchyard a pair of great

wrought iron gates leads into the grounds. Tall, unkempt trees and shrubs, and the rear of the now empty house tower darkly above you in a weird, theatrical way. A rotting notice board, half hidden in a bush, informs those of the faith when the chapel in the house is open for mass. Chickens scrabble in the undergrowth, the grass sprouts from the gravel and as the sun sets behind a chilly cloud we begin to feel unwelcome here. It is time to return to our snug cabin before the pale dead rise with the evening mists. All this is too much part of a dream of long ago when equality was nothing, quality everything, when great adventures were afoot, when men could prance and pray, and poets sang for all to hear.

For the next two miles to Pangbourne and Whitchurch the river is wide and straight, the countryside open and pleasant. On the way we pass famous HARDWICKE HOUSE on the right, set well back from the river but plain to see. The core and foundations of the house are probably of the 14th century but it has been much altered at different times. Apart from the arched colonnade the general character is Tudor more than anything else with its many gables and stone-mullioned windows. Part of it is of the 17th century and a whole wing was added at the beginning of this century. Queen Elizabeth stayed here on one of her Progresses and a bed-room bearing her name is believed to have been specially decorated for her coming. In 1647 Charles I was a prisoner for three weeks at Caversham Lodge but was allowed to come here 'attended by Colonel Rossiter's troop of horse', when he played bowls on the hill behind the house. It was later badly damaged during the fighting when it lay between the two garrisons at Wallingford and Reading from out of which rode plundering troops. The estate has been a family seat since the Conquest when it was owned by the De Herdewyke family. In 1730 it came by marriage into the hands of a family called Powys from which sprang a son who married a girl called Caroline. She became Mrs. Lybbe-Powys, the indefatigable diarist to whom we have already referred. She kept this diary from 1756 to 1808 and in it gives us a fascinating glimpse of the life in the Thames Valley at that time. She loved her riverside home as deeply as she loved her amiable husband and gives much information about both in her writings.

PANGBOURNE is known for its nautical college and for being
the birthplace of Kenneth Grahame of *The Wind in the Willows*,
the famous children's book with its strong upper Thames atmosphere. The church has a good brick tower of the 18th century
and an interesting Elizabethan monument to Sir John Davis
concealed behind the organ, but otherwise the place has little
of interest.

WHITCHURCH on the Oxfordshire side, however, is a very
pretty place with its mill and pond and its street of cottages
rising up the hill to an ancient inn. The church with a timber
tower is partly Norman but much restored. At Whitchurch was
born the famous architect Sir John Soane.

The toll bridge is no beauty but it is well to remember the
saying that bridges are less things to cross or to admire than
things to stand on and look over. Stand and look over this
bridge, then, at the approach to Whitchurch Lock, for the
picture is attractive. Tall overhanging trees line the cut and
there at the end are the lock gates, small, white and precise,
a perfect foil to the dark water and the untramelled foliage.

A road runs along parallel with the river on the Berkshire
side for about a mile beyond Pangbourne, while in Oxfordshire
the grounds of Coombe Park come down to the river. Beyond
lie HARTSLOCK WOODS and the Oxfordshire Downs begin—as
fine a reach as any on the river. Here the limestone mansion of
BASILDON PARK can be seen about half a mile away among
the woods in Berkshire. It was built in 1767 to designs by John
Carr of York (1723-1807) in the grand manner of the 18th
century which invariably sought inspiration from the Italian,
Andrea Palladio. The architects of the time went in frankly
for show rather than use or domestic convenience and brought
from Pope his well-known protest:

'Tis very fine,
But where d'ye sleep, or where d'ye dine?
I see from all you have been telling
That 'tis a house, but not a dwelling.

Carr was a good architect but always kept to the correct
classical rules. Apart from Basildon he worked only in the
north where his most famous building is Harewood House. The

main elevation of Basildon, which faces away from the river, has a central block with a grand portico flanked on either side by smaller blocks, all being held together by a rusticated ground floor. These Palladian houses were always plain and formal outside but highly decorated within, and Basildon is no exception. It has plasterwork of two periods, the first by Carr, carried out when the house was built, the second by John Papworth of about 1838. Papworth (1775-1847) is known for his charming books illustrated with aquatints of specimen rustic cottages and suburban villas, but he also did a fair amount of work, largely of a decorative nature. Among other things he redecorated the inside of Boodle's Club and also laid out a large part of the model town of Cheltenham. Besides some of the plasterwork, he carried out other work at Basildon—additions to the house, much interior detailing such as overmantels, and also the refined, ornate and almost baroque entrance gates and lodges, which are perhaps the best of Basildon and can be seen by everyone from the road.

In midstream at this part of the river are a number of eyots and between one of these and the Oxfordshire bank a flash lock existed for many centuries, known as Hart's at least as long ago as the 16th century. Its piles were still there in 1910 when they were removed as a nuisance. The Harts seem to have been a very old and prolific river family whose name we shall come across again.

Near the river stands BASILDON CHURCH which, though uninteresting in itself, helps to form with the neighbouring vicarage and farm buildings a comely group. A Victorian writer informs us that within sight of these buildings an osier farm once flourished. Osier farming was a distinct riverside industry supplying the raw material for wicker baskets and chairs. It seems to have now completely died out, and it might be of interest, therefore, to record what our informant saw of the workings of this industry. 'Out of the river', he writes,

formal growths of tall green sheaves seem to flourish within a ring fence. There is a rude building, half shed and half cottage, at the mouth of the gully, and in an open space between it and the Thames men, women and children are working. Proceeding down the path the mystery gradually unfolds. We are facing an osier farm. The tall slender sheaves are bundles of withies that have been reaped from

156

the islands and osier beds, and punted *en masse* in the water, and the cut branches make the best they can of divorcement from the parent root, and preserve their vitality until they are required for use. The girls and boys are very handy at the operation of peeling. They take up a withy from the bundle last landed from the pound, draw it rapidly through a couple of pieces of iron fixed to a stand, and in a twinkling the bright green osier has become a snow-white wand.

Beyond the second of Brunel's simple but noble brick railway bridges, the river makes a bold sweep round to the right, passing on the Berkshire side a house called THE GROTTO because here, before the house was built (c. 1810), Lady Fane of Basildon Park erected one of those 'divine grots' embellished with shells and corals which were so dear to the 18th century. Here we are passing through the GORING GAP where maybe the Chilterns and the Berkshire Downs once joined before either a sudden upheaval or the infinite patience of rain through thousands of centuries had worked a new passage for the upper river which had hitherto been content to flow not eastwards to the North Sea but further north to join the Great Ouse on its way to the Wash. It is possible that a great lake then spread over the land above Goring. But all this is speculation.

About a mile beyond Basildon Railway Bridge we reach the long bridge linking the small town of GORING, situated in one of the Chiltern Hundreds called Langtree, with the large village of STREATLEY in Berkshire. The scene is whole and serene with its mill streams (the old Streatley mill has gone but the Goring mill remains), its long weir and foaming lasher, its two church towers, its tree-clad eyots and its tidy lock (the only lock on the river, besides Boulter's, possessing a secondary compartment). Just above the lock we can turn back up a mill stream to a snug mooring for which a small fee is charged. Thence on foot to explore the town and replenish stores, not forgetting to buy fresh, warm bread in the main street straight from the baker's oven.

The church of Goring (*Garinges* in the *Domesday Book*) is even more mixed in Gothic styles than most country churches. Originally built at the end of the 11th century it later served as an Augustinian convent founded during the reign of Henry II. The north aisle was added about 1200 and the whole was remodelled about a hundred years later. The apse is Victorian.

Its old bells are famous and one of them has sounded across the valley here for over six hundred years.

Streatley, being further from the railway station, is more picturesque and rural than Goring though it possesses nothing of outstanding architectural interest. The church is partly Transitional between Norman and Early English with a 15th-century tower and, though greatly restored in the last century, its squat proportions are agreeable and from a distance epitomise every English country church that was ever built. In the sloping main street stands a large Georgian mansion now belonging to the Royal Veterinary College. Streatley, meaning the ley or meadow by the road, derives its name from the Icknield Way which passed through the village and crossed the river by a causeway in the days of the Roman Occupation. Though it was used by the Romans as part of their highway system it was a road long before they came for it was originally one of those grassy ridge-ways of the high grounds which formed the country-wide network of the Stone Age men when the valleys were mostly impenetrable swamp.

The main virtue of Streatley is its hill which is now preserved by the National Trust. The climb to the top is well worth the effort for the view of the valley up there is magnificent—distant hills, farmland, parks and woods through which the river winds its way, marked by a fringe of willow trees and poplars, while in the foreground just below us the old colourful village nestles happily among its foliage. Take no notice of the advice of the Lazy Minstrel who wrote those verses on Streatley which appeared in *Punch* many decades ago, and which have appeared in so many Thames guide books since. Why should the tradition be broken now?

> Ah! Here I am! I've drifted down—
> The Sun is hot, my face is brown—
> Before the wind from Moulsford Down,
>   So pleasantly and fleetly!
> I am not certain what's o'clock,
> And so I won't go through the lock;
> But wisely steer the *Shuttlecock*
>   Beside the 'Swan' at Streatley!

Beyond Reading the river's lost serenity returns. Once more the trees encompass us, as in the approach to Whitchurch Lock, BELOW, where the white precision of the lock gates makes a perfect foil to the dark walls of the untrammelled trees. Past the fine reach by Hartslock Woods and through the Goring Gap, we reach the friendly settlements of Goring and Streatley. Goring has a millstream along which, RIGHT, lies a boatyard with a rhythmical row of gables.

TOP LEFT, a calm retreat on the Goring millstream. BELOW LEFT, the *Swan Inn* at Streatley. ABOVE, the weir machinery at Goring Lock, purely functional and yet, in its white paint and rhythmical repetition, it helps, like other Thames furniture, to create the pleasant river style. RIGHT, the dramatic arches of Moulsford Railway Bridge below Goring, one of Brunel's brick trio—the only railway bridges of the Thames which do not break the harmony of the river's visual character.

TOP LEFT, Cleeve Lock cottage, one of
the oldest on the river. BELOW LEFT,
a sultry afternoon lures children to play
by the river below Wallingford Bridge.
ABOVE, Wallingford Bridge, a very old
one, rebuilt several times; these three
central arches date from 1809; here by
the bridge is a meadow where bathing
can be enjoyed in a natural unregimented
way. RIGHT, the fascinating pierced
spire of St. Peter's, built in the 1770s,
is the focus of the riverside picture at
Wallingford.

LEFT, a Georgian coaching inn, *The Castle* at Benson, with its fine wrought-iron sign frame; Benson was a mid-way stop between Henley and Oxford in coaching days, an important stage on the London to Oxford run. BELOW, the lawn and swimming pool of the *Shillingford Bridge Hotel*, an admirable example of how to create a public riverside bathing place of an artificial nature.

ABOVE, a natural bathing place where a village street comes down to the river at Shillingford. BELOW, the prehistoric earthworks of the Sinodun Hills; no one knows who dug them but they were probably there long before the Romans came.

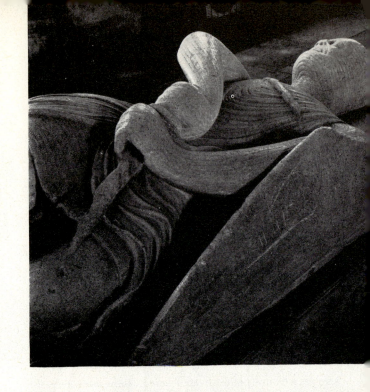

LEFT, two beautiful medieval relics in Dorchester Abbey Church; TOP, the Dancing Knight, an unknown warrier, defiant even in death; BELOW, the graceful Madonna of the 14th-century fresco in the chancel. THIS PAGE, ABOVE, the Georgian mansion at Culham seen through its wrought-iron gates. BELOW, Clifton Hampden Bridge seen from the porch of the small church on the cliff; a towering lombardy poplar, in contrast to the horizontal line of the bridge, makes a typical Thames scene.

Abingdon is the queen of
Thames towns. ABOVE LEFT,
the approach view dominated
by the perpendicular spire of
St Helen's. ABOVE RIGHT, the
County Hall of 1783. BELOW,
the Brick Alley Almshouses and
the spire of St Helen's with its
flying buttresses. FACING
PAGE, TOP, a medieval townscape in East St Helen's Street.
BELOW, Abingdon Bridge, built in 1416 but restored in the 1920's.

Now we are nearing Oxford. On the way lies Sandford in whose small church hangs a Thames-side treasure—a medieval alabaster carving of the Assumption of the Virgin, LEFT. BELOW, a modern convenience and, except for its fussy railings, a beautiful one—the concrete footbridge above Iffley.

ABOVE, the approach to Iffley Lock with its grand informal tree-scape. BELOW, the college barges at Oxford along Christ Church Meadow.

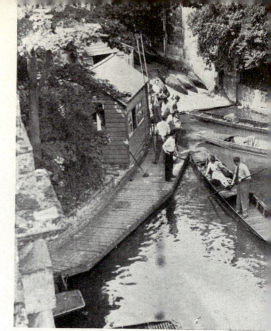

FACING PAGE, TOP RIGHT, the boat station at Magdalen Bridge, Oxford.
TOP LEFT, the figurehead of the college barge displaced from Oxford and
now lying by the swimming pool at Shillingford Bridge. BELOW LEFT,
a close-up of the college barges—'the oddest little street, this row of motley
Noah's Arks'. ABOVE, the workshop of a thriving riverside industry at
Oxford, where Mr. Collar and his men make the oars, paddles and poles
for the small pleasure boats of the river.

173

The River Cherwell seen from Magdalen Bridge, Oxford, with its effect of a mysterious miniature Amazon. We have now seen enough of the river to have understood that special Thames *cachet* for whose preservation and enhancement the author pleads in Chapter 6. The essential style of the river to be preserved consists of its winding linear form which makes it a unique strip-park, its sense of remoteness and escape from the outer world, whether screened by foliage like the scene above or opened out to broad landscape, its sudden swift surprises and rapid contrasts as between informal, verdant rusticity and gay, decorative urbanity, both of which possess qualities peculiar to the Thames alone.

And when you're here, I'm told that you
Should mount the Hill and see the view;
And gaze and wonder, if you'd do
   Its merits most completely:
The air is clear, the sky is fine,
The prospect is, I know, divine—
But most distinctly I decline
   To climb the Hill at Streatley!

But from the Hill I understand
You gaze across rich pasture land,
And fancy you see Oxford and
   P'raps Wallingford and Wheatley:
Upon the winding Thames you gaze,
And though the view's beyond all praise,
I'd rather much sit here and laze
   Than scale the Hill at Streatley!

From Goring Lock to CLEEVE LOCK is just over half a mile —the shortest pound on the river. It is followed by the longest pound. The next lock at Benson is six and a half miles away, which is why trial eights find this a convenient training ground. Cleeve Lock has a happy, sunny character and possesses one of the oldest, if not the oldest, of existing lock cottages. This is the place to capture one of those rare but unforgettable moods of contentment—to stretch out full length by the towpath and gaze up into a cloudless sky. Not a soul is about, the larks' monotonous song and the insects' buzz add to the silence. The sun blesses our inert bodies with a power that is more than warmth. A river steamer appears, hissing gently, while a piano tinkles and the people sing. We rise to lend a hand with the paddles and return the badinage. 'A real gin and winkle do', murmurs the grinning lock keeper. Soon the steamer churns away into the summer haze, the lock keeper retires to his garden behind the cottage, quietness returns and we resume a state of torpor in the hay. The sense of remoteness comes back but more fully than before by contrast with the noisy interruption. A typical example, this, of one of the river advantages on which the author digressed in the last chapter—of how the river can be enjoyed either in gay company or in solitary contemplation. Neither pleasure destroys the other but rather enhances it, for in this long Thames park there is space to spare.

A short way beyond Cleeve Lock on the right stands *The
Leather Bottel* (*sic*) *Inn* below an embankment, near which a
medicinal spring once issued from 'a fat, whitish earth' as Dr.
Plot, writing in the time of Charles II, informs us—'a very good
remedy for the ach of Corns, and some other such remedies'
including ulcers and sore eyes. Further along on the Berkshire
side lies another inn called *The Beetle and Wedge*, the beetle
being no insect but a wooden mallet for driving in a wedge
when cleaving a log of wood. Here a ferry plies between the
villages of MOULSFORD and SOUTH STOKE. Both have charm
but unless you wish to stretch your legs, they are hardly worth
visiting. Beyond the ferry we pass on the left, first Moulsford
Manor, now a hotel, and then, very close to the river, the small
14th-century church of St. John the Baptist, which, though
restored, still looks delightful with its shingled spire rising above
the weeping willows.

Ahead the brickwork of MOULSFORD RAILWAY BRIDGE,
the last of Brunel's trio, leaps with long, strong strides across
the water. As you pass under the cool vault look up and along.
The effect is remarkable. Clearly a second bridge was added
to the first when the railway grew in importance and the two
were linked by small transverse arches which give architectural
counterpoint and a grand scale to the structure. The effect is
no doubt quite accidental, yet has something of that deliberately conceived dramatic power you find in Piranesi's architectural etchings.

Pleasant, if uneventful, scenery continues for a mile or two,
marred only by the grim silhouette of the Berkshire Mental
Hospital up on a slope—one of those monstrous institutions
with which the Victorians frightened and punished themselves
and depressed posterity. We pass NORTH STOKE VILLAGE on
our right, screened by trees. Here is a Gothic church with an
18th-century tower which contains some biblical wall paintings
in the nave and a good Jacobean pulpit. Beyond, also on the
Oxfordshire side, is MONGEWELL PARK. The house itself is
hidden behind trees but that is of no consequence, for the house
is of this century and now acts as an R.A.F. rehabilitation
centre. The little early Gothik Revival tower of the church in
the grounds, however, is clearly visible from the river and helps
to make a picture, though the church as a whole is now a ruin.

The grounds with its lake are old and lovely. The place was at one time an episcopal retreat for the Bishops of Durham but the mansion was burned down—by angry villagers so gossip says—after which the lady of the house committed suicide. If willing to delve, one would probably find a tragic human story in these events.

The grounds with its lake are old and lovely. The place was at one time an episcopal retreat for the Bishops of Durham but the mansion was burned down—by angry villagers so gossip says—after which the lady of the house committed suicide. If willing to delve, one would probably find a tragic human story in these events.

Just beyond Mongewell is a section of that mysterious earthwork known as GRIM'S DITCH or Dyke (Grim being the Devil) which runs for several miles along the hills towards Henley. It continues with breaks into Herts and Bucks for a distance of fifty miles. No one knows exactly who made it and various theories about its origin are held. One theory believes that it was dug slightly before the 7th century as a boundary mark between Wessex and Mercia, another that it is an early line of defence, a third that it is a Roman *vallum*.

The approach to WALLINGFORD BRIDGE is pleasing on account of the gardens coming down to the river, the Georgian houses they serve and the quaint, pierced stone spire of St. Peter's Church built by Sir Robert Taylor in the 1770s. It is in the Gothik manner but somehow it looks rather classical reminding one of Wren's city church of St. Bride's in Fleet Street. The Victorians considered the spire to be a revolting object but nowadays we like it—which goes to show how unstable are the canons of taste. The bridge is a fine old structure of many arches and, like so many of our churches, is a composite of several different periods. Part of it goes right back to the 13th century, other parts belong to the 16th and 18th centuries while the three centre arches are of 1809. Originally there was a wooden structure here and before that, as the name of the town implies, there was only a ford.

WALLINGFORD, which may mean either the Walled Ford or the ford of the Wallingas, the sons of the Welsh (as the British were then called), is another of those Thames towns which are served only by a branch railway line. Thus they have preserved their peaceful quality and avoided the squalors of modern expansion. This is a small, sleepy country town, though it was once, as we have seen, one of the most important centres on the river—a vital crossing point. Britons, Romans, Saxons and Danes have all had their settlements at Wallingford. Here the Britons fought with Aulus Plautius, lieutenant

of Claudius, over the passage of the river; and here William
the Conqueror received the submission of a man called Wiggod
before crossing over on his march to occupy London; here
the Empress Maud was besieged by King Stephen and here
Henry II held his first Parliament. After the Conquest Robert
d'Oigly, the first Norman Governor of Oxford, had been given
the job of building a castle here on the site of a Roman fort.
He did the job well for the Castle survived a number of terrible
assaults until Fairfax managed to wreck it with some difficulty
in the Civil War. Now it is a mere pile of rubble which can
just be seen from the river above the bridge. The town was
well defended long before the Conquest, however, as the earth
ramparts with their moats, which can still be seen along the
west, north and south sides of the town, give proof. These were
no doubt used by the Romans but they were probably built
by the Britons—perhaps by the Berkshire tribe of the Atrebates, whose chief city this may have been. At the time of the
Domesday Survey Wallingford was a royal borough, the largest
in Berkshire, and during the 11th and 12th centuries possessed
no less than fourteen churches. But in 1348 the Black Death
almost depopulated the town. This frightful event, coupled
with the growing importance of Abingdon and the building of
other bridges, greatly reduced the importance of the place until
its fourteen churches were finally reduced to the present three.

Of these three, St. Leonard's on the south-east of the town
is the most interesting, for its herring-bone masonry indicates
that it is pre-Conquest. Inside are two Norman arches and
much Victorian addition. In the Market Place is a town hall
of 1670 supported on Doric pillars and containing a grand oak
staircase. There are also a number of good houses in the town
from Tudor to Georgian, including Bridge House on the river
front near the bridge, designed, like the tower and spire of the
church of St. Peter, by Sir Robert Taylor. Below it, also on the
river front, is Castle Priory House, now a hotel, built several
decades earlier in the middle of the 18th century.

On the Oxfordshire bank opposite Wallingford lies the
village of CROWMARSH GIFFORD which has a small Norman
church with a massive vestry door of oak, formerly in the west
wall, which is said to bear the marks of Roundhead bullets.

Above the bridge on the right is a public bathing place laid out in the dull way so typical of municipal design and then we pass on the same side the grounds of Howbery Park. An Elizabethan manor stood there up to the late 18th century when the present house was erected. After a mile or so of field, willow and withy, we reach BENSON LOCK and then, just above the lock in Oxfordshire, Benson itself. A stop here is recommended, not just to see the village but to take a walk (if you miss one of the rare buses) to Ewelme lying about two miles 'inland'. Ewelme should not be missed for it is one of the sights, not merely of the Thames Valley, but of the whole of England.

BENSON, or, to give the full title, Bensington, was important in coaching days as the mid-way stage between Henley and Oxford on the London to Oxford run, though the village goes back at least fifteen centuries. It was noted at one time for its saddlery and coach-building (hence its Brummagem Yard) and here some of the earliest railway carriages in the country were made. It has three attractive 18th-century inns and a much restored church with an 18th-century tower, in which is set a clock bought second hand in 1794 from the Horse Guards, London, for £50. Inside is a Norman font with a Jacobean cover and a monument with a curious epitaph which is worth recording:

M.S.

To the pious memory
of Ralph Quelch and Jane his wife

who slept } together in 1 { bed by ye space of 40 yeares.
now sleepe } { grave till Ct. shall awaken them.

He } fell asleep Ano. Dni. { 1629 } being aged { 63 } yeares.
She } { 1619 } { 59 }

For ye fruit of their { labours } they left { ye new inn twice built at their own charge.
{ bodies } { one only son and two daughters.

Their son being liberally bred in ye University of Oxon thought himself bound
to erect this small monument

of { their } piety towards { God
{ his } { them

Ano. Dni. 16 . .

To EWELME now by road passing on the way an airfield on whose perimeter stands a magnificent, great Victorian barn. The village is a delight. It surrounds a watercress farm but is more famous for its group of flint and brick buildings comprising the school, almshouses and church—all of the 15th century.

The name comes from Aewilme which is Saxon for the spring in the hollow. The spring which is fresh, clear and good for drinking, rises near the church and then trickles down to feed the watercress beds. Chaucer, who must have visited his son here, may well have had Ewelme spring in mind when he wrote:

> In world is none more clere in hewe,
> Its water ever fresh and newe,
> That whelmeth up in wavis breighte
> Its mountenance of two fingers heighte.

The best of the group of old buildings are the courtyard of the almshouses (called God's House) and the monuments in the church. From the courtyard with its central well and its covered way of brick and timber which forms a small, intimate cloister, a well-worn stairway leads up into the church. These almshouses and the school attached to them were founded in 1437 when Henry VI granted to William de la Pole, Duke of Suffolk, and to Alice, his wife, 'that they, or either survivors of them, found an Hospital at their Manor of Ewelme, in the County of Oxford, and settle a sufficient endowment, not exceeding the yearly value of 200 marks, for the maintenance of two Chaplains and thirteen poor men to be incorporated and to have a Common Seal.' One of the chaplains was to be called Master of the Almshouse and the other Teacher of Grammar. In 1513, the Crown took over all the Suffolk family estates including Ewelme and in 1605, James I passed the Mastership of the Almshouse to the Regius Professor of Medicine (Physic, they used to call it) at Oxford—an arrangement which still prevails. The office of Grammar Master has been dropped and his house is now occupied by the local schoolmaster.

The interior of the church is beautiful and in a fine state of preservation for it escaped Roundhead mutilation. For this thanks are due to a local inhabitant, Colonel Francis Martyn, who held a high command in Cromwell's army and would not permit any soldiery to enter the place except during divine service. The first thing to notice is the carved roofwork and the corbel carvings below; next, the octagonal 15th-century font with its contemporary cover splendidly carved in wood, over ten feet high and surmounted by a figure of St. Michael. It is

*At Ewelme. The Almshouse courtyard, left, and winged figures on the tomb
of Alice, Duchess of Suffolk, right*

considered to be the finest of its kind in the country. Examine
then the remarkable alabaster tomb on the south of the sanctuary of Alice, Duchess of Suffolk. She died in 1475 and the tomb
was probably made soon afterwards at the flourishing School of
Sculpture at Nottingham. The cornice of the canopy is elabor-
ately carved with formal decoration surmounting a row of
winged figures. Above this, on stone columns, four carved wood
figures stand sentinel. The tomb itself is in three tiers—first the
recumbent effigy of the Duchess, a masterpiece of formal sculpture; then the tomb chest decorated with heraldic figures and
containing her remains; below that an area enclosed by an
arcade within which lies an emaciated, shrouded figure representing the Duchess in death ('Ogglesome', Dickens calls it in
his *Dictionary*). The ceiling of this compartment is decorated
with brightly coloured frescoes still in an excellent condition,
as you can see if you lie on your back on the floor beside the
monument. An interesting feature of the effigy of the Duchess
is that it wears on the left forearm the Garter of St. George.
Only two other female effigies ever received this honour, one
of them being that of Lady Harcourt at Stanton Harcourt
which we shall come to above Oxford.

Another good tomb here is the brass monument to Thomas
Chaucer, Lord of the Manor, who was the Duchess's father and
the son of Geoffrey Chaucer, the poet, and to his wife Matilda,
a lady who had a family connection with Richard II. Thomas
died in 1434, having been an important man in his time—

among other things Constable of Wallingford Castle, Butler to Henry V, whom he supported in combat at Agincourt, seven times Member of Parliament for Oxfordshire and, in 1414, Speaker of the House of Commons. His daughter Alice took, as her third husband, the Earl of Suffolk and with him built the church, school and almshouse here. This man has been painted a traitor, in particular by Shakespeare, but if all the truth were known, it might be found that he did not in the least deserve that brutal, unceremonious beheading by a sailor with a rusty sword on the gunwhale of a boat at Dover beach.

There are a number of other monuments in the church. One not to be missed is that on the north wall of the sanctuary to Henry, son of the Earl of Barkshire, 1647. It has a quaint fascination of form, being an urn of baked clay from which the spirit of the deceased issues forth assisted by two angels. There are many fine brasses in the church, too. Outside in the churchyard lies buried Jerome K. Jerome.

The Palace of Ewelme no longer exists but it was a royal residence in the times of Henry VIII and Elizabeth. A lane in the village is still known as Queen Elizabeth's Walk and part of the watercress bed is called King's Pool. A local legend says that Anne Boleyn pushed Henry into this pool one day when his carnal desire was becoming too active for her liking. Perhaps it was on that occasion that she informed him that the way to her bedchamber lay through the Throne Room.

The reach from Benson to SHILLINGFORD BRIDGE is a fine one, wide open on the Oxfordshire side and developing to a cliff on the Berkshire bank, below which, when you reach the pleasing brick and stone bridge of 1827, stretches the wide lawn of the *Shillingford Bridge Hotel* with its simple, rectangular swimming pool. A good view can be obtained from the bridge down stream with this lawn in the foreground sweeping cleanly to the river and backed by a screen of lombardies. A brightly painted college barge with dragon's head prow, which has been displaced from Oxford, forms a decorative point of interest and helps to wed the site to the river. This is an ideal solution of the riverside bathing place which the local authorities might well try to emulate.

Beyond a twist in the river Shillingford Village touches the water and then beyond another twist the twin hills of Sinodun with their characteristic and fascinating spinneys of beech called the WITTENHAM CLUMPS, come well into view. The reason why they are known unofficially as the Berkshire Bubs is now apparent. Up this reach on our right the little RIVER THAME, having drained most of the Vale of Aylesbury, joins the parent stream. There is an old legend that the river above this point is really called Isis and that the word Thames is a composite of Thame and Isis, but that is just a poet's fancy. Warton and Drayton have sung of this legend but before them Spenser wrote in his *Faërie Queen:*

> The lovely bridegroom came,
> The noble Thamis, with all his goodly traine,
> But before him there went, as best became,
>   His auncient parents, namely, th' auncient Thame;
> But much more aged was his wife than he,
>   The Ouze, whom men doe Isis rightly name.
> Full weak and crooked creature seemed shee,
> And almost blind through Eld, that scarce her way could see.

Just past a wood we shall find a quiet mooring where the river gives a surprising turn sharply to the right close by LITTLE WITTENHAM village. Now we must climb the SINODUN HILL, the most notable landmark on the upper river which can be seen from miles around, and from which a great panorama of unspoiled country can be viewed. Moreover the system of earthworks, especially those round the eastern clump, is worth inspecting and will set your mind romancing about their long past. This great system of fortifications of ramparts and ditches, together with the two earth banks across the river called the Dyke Hills running between the Thames and the Thame, was once thought to be the work of the Atrebates behind which they defended their camp for the last time against Julius Caesar. That theory has been destroyed and whether the Britons, the Romans, or the Danes dug them no one really knows. Hilaire Belloc suggests that they were held from the very beginning of human habitation in this district as a permanent fortress into which the neighbouring tribes could retire during war. He suggests also that the Dyke Hills formed an outlying bastion needed for protection when the river was low and fordable.

Let us stroll now across Day's Lock to Dorchester whose

church and roofs we can see across the fields half a mile distant, We can drop into LITTLE WITTENHAM church on the way, to see its interesting brasses. DORCHESTER is historically one of the most interesting towns on the river and there are some matchless things to see in the church there too. Dorchester is another quiet little place which was once great and splendid. The name comes from the Celtic *Dorcics* with the Latin *castra*, or camp, tagged on, showing that it was a fortified Roman town and a settlement before the Romans came. St. Birinus came here to preach from Italy in the year 635 and here he baptized Cynegils, the first West Saxon king to be converted. From then until 1092 Dorchester was at the most flourishing period of its history, because not only was it the capital of Wessex but it was also the centre of an enormous episcopal see comprising the kingdoms of the West Saxons and the Mercians—a place where twenty bishops sat in papal grandeur. The Venerable Bede visited it in the 8th century and tells us that then *Civitas Dorcinia* was full of richly garnished churches. After the Conquest the dioceses were reorganised, the bishopric was removed to Lincoln and Dorchester dwindled in importance. Nevertheless an Augustinian priory was founded at Dorchester in 1140 and a new church was built on the site of the old cathedral, parts of which still exist in the one standing today.

This abbey church happily survived the Dissolution when it was purchased by Richard Bewforest for £140 and presented to the parish. It is remarkable for its great length and its patchwork of styles from the twelfth century to the seventeenth. It was partly 'restored', of course, by Sir Gilbert Scott but luckily funds ran out and less damage was caused than had been planned.

We enter the church by a wooden porch of the 11th century protecting a doorway of the 13th and find ourselves not in the main church but in the chancel which was formerly reserved for the monks at a time when the nave was the public place of worship. The east wall of this chancel bears the remains of a fading fresco of the 14th century—Christ on the cross flanked by St. John on the right side and the Madonna on the left. It is a lovely, simple, graceful relic. In the south aisle is a Norman font, one of the very few lead fonts in England. It is decorated with eleven of the apostles seated under arches (Judas being excluded) and it has a strongly Byzantine character. The chief pride of the church, however, is the rare and world-famous 14th-century Jesse window in the north wall of the sanctuary. In its glass and its stone carving it shows the genealogical Tree of Jesse, springing from the body of Jesse himself. Other stone effigies represent members of the royal house of David leading up to the crowning figure of Christ, which has been virtually destroyed, possibly by Cromwell's soldiery.*

The best thing in Dorchester Abbey Church to the author's mind is not the Jesse Window, however, but the recumbent figure of the unknown warrior in the south aisle, a stone crusader worn by time to a smooth, polished patina. The figure is one of those rare Dancing Knights, so called on account of their vigorous attitudes. This fellow has his knee raised and his hand lies on the handle of his sword as though he were about to leap shouting into battle. He seems to be undefeated by death, and even the despoilers who smashed his nose have not been able to make him lie still; indeed, they seem merely to have increased the pugnacious look of his bullet head. This is a grand and powerful piece of sculpture, an ancient Henry Moore.

Near the unknown warrior lies another knight. He, too, is recumbent, but he rests quietly there by the choir screen and his name *is* known. He is Gilbert Lord Segrave, Governor of Wallingford, who died about 1400. This alabaster monument is of exceptional craftsmanship.

* A Tree of Jesse has been defined as the representation of a recumbent figure from whose body rises a tree. On this appear some of the ancestors of Christ and at the summit Christ Himself. But that is a broad definition. In the period from the end of the 11th to the end of the 12th century Christian imagery developed from simple to highly complex forms of which the Tree of Jesse is one example. The Tree is found represented, as at Dorchester, in stone carving and stained glass, in illuminated manuscripts, in wood carving and so on. The imagery is based on Matthew i, 6-16: 'And Jesse begat David the king . . . And David begat Joseph the husband of Mary, of whom was born Jesus, who is called Christ'; and on Isaiah xi, 1-3: 'And there shall come forth a rod out of the stem of Jesse, and a Branch shall grow out of his roots: and the spirit of the Lord shall rest upon him, the spirit of wisdom and understanding, the spirit of counsel and might, the spirit of knowledge and of the fear of the Lord.' The theme varies and it is not of its essence that the figure of Jesse should be recumbent or that it should have an explicit genealogical *motif*; prophets and kings are often represented and Christ and the Virgin are sometimes represented, not in human, but in symbolic forms.

Another monument, which is inserted in the floor of the monks' chancel, is also worth noting, not so much for its design as for its curious inscription:

Reader! If thou hast a Heart fam'd for Tenderness and Pity, Contemplate this Spot. In which are deposited the remains of a Young Lady, whose artless Beauty, innocence of Mind, and gentle Manners, once obtained for her the Love and Esteem of all who knew her. But when Nerves were too delicately spun to bear the rude Shakes and Jostlings which we meet with in this transitory World, Nature gave way; She sunk and died a Martyr to Excessive Sensibility. Mrs. SARAH FLETCHER, Wife of Captain FLETCHER, dyparted this life at the Village of Clifton on the 7 of June, 1799. In the 29 Year of her Age. May her Soul meet that Peace in Heaven which this Earth denied her.

Conditioned as we now are by modern psychological jargon could we hope to approach in our age such tender, sympathetic wording?

From DAY'S LOCK the river begins a horse-shoe sweep northwards and then takes a great winding detour to the west so that, although a crow has only a three-mile flight from Day's to the Lock Cottage at Nuneham Park, the journey by river between these two points is over ten miles. Beyond the lock on the right below some pollard willows is a splendid mooring place with deep water and a most pleasing view all round, especially southwards where the Bubs stand up darkly against the sky—a place for fishing, bathing and just lingering. Two and a half miles brings us to the village of CLIFTON HAMPDEN containing some pretty thatched cottages, a small church on a cliff and a red brick bridge of 1864 with Gothic arches by Sir Gilbert Scott—one of his better designs. Scott was also responsible for the restoration of the church—originally a chapel served from Dorchester Abbey. This restoration was one of Scott's earliest jobs and thanks partly to its perched position and its frame of trees has a quaint character which adds to the unique atmosphere of the place. Here among the bright, tall hollyhocks of a cottage garden one hopes to meet a little girl in a starched white pinafore and with golden hair falling below a round, flopping, cotton hat trimmed with pink ribbons. Then the rustic idyll of a Victorian oleograph would be complete. The village is, indeed, strangely isolated—so much so that its people find the pleasure steamers a valuable transport utility.

A short way down the road from the bridge on the Berkshire side is the old BARLEY MOW INN, where one hot summer evening the author enjoyed his first taste of a long and wonderful drink recommended by the host—sparkling, ice-cold cider laced with gin. The inn, of timber crutch construction with a thatched roof, dates back to 1350. Here Jerome K. Jerome stayed awhile, finding it a 'fairy tale inn', and here William Dyke once drank good local beer—the man who fired the first shot at Waterloo. He did so without orders and was demoted, but when Wellington afterwards visited Lord Harcourt at Nuneham Park a few miles away he heard about Dyke and returned his sword to him.

A few hundred yards above the bridge is CLIFTON LOCK, to the left of which runs a backwater. Up there we can tie up and visit LONG WITTENHAM. This is truly a very long village and straggles for nearly a mile down the road. It was partly destroyed by fire in 1868 and the subsequent rebuilding has not added to its attraction. Nevertheless it is still quite charming and its church is worth seeing. One enters it on the south through a carved timber porch with ornamented barge boards. It is of the Perpendicular period and is believed to have come from Lincoln Cathedral at a time when the church was under the Lincoln diocese. The church, like that at Dorchester, contains a rare font of lead which was once so carefully hidden from the Roundheads that it could not be found for two hundred years afterwards. It is at least eight centuries old and is the only lead font on its original stone base in existence. Another item of the interior is the piscina in the south chapel which bears some extremely fine 13th-century stone carving of trefoils, angels and a minute effigy, only two feet long, of a knight in armour standing on a serpent.

For nearly three miles above Clifton Lock the landscape is rather dull and flat on both sides, which are linked near Appleford by an ugly iron railway viaduct. Then we come to the simple stone road bridge of Sutton. Let us land here to see both CULHAM in Oxfordshire and Sutton Courtenay in Berkshire. Culham Church is of no interest but the village contains two beautiful old houses. Opposite the church is the Manor House, whose stone walls and mullioned windows tell us that the Cotswold country is near. Its bountiful old garden is decorated with topiary. The other house is Culham House which can be seen from the green through intricate wrought iron gates. It stands well back, a noble, symmetrical, Georgian palace of red brick and white paintwork.

SUTTON COURTENAY is a lovely village both in its general effect and in its individual buildings. Its backwater is generally held to be the most beautiful on the river with its Sutton Pool and deep lasher catching the water from the weirs among the willows. The village contains so many old houses that it can be regarded as a museum of English domestic architecture. The houses include Norman Hall, a 12th-century stone building and one of the two oldest inhabited houses in Berkshire; the Manor House, once the home of the Courtenays and interesting as an example of a gabled Tudor building; the Abbey, largely of the 14th century with a fine hall, once a cell or grange belonging to the monks of Abingdon. The house which the author finds most appealing, however, is that which lies on the south side of the main village street—a simple brick Georgian building with good detailing which includes over the entrance door a canopy decorated with intricate plasterwork.

The church facing a spacious green is composed of Gothic styles ranging from the 12th to the 16th centuries. The best things here are the open timber roof and the royal coat of arms of Charles II painted large and bold over the chancel arch with the commandments on either side. In the churchyard is a 14th-century altar tomb, a headstone to a Mrs. Martha Pye who died in 1822 at the age of 117 years, and a yew tree about two hundred and fifty years old which must have been planted when Mrs. Pye was very young.

From the end of Culham Cut northwards we continue for a mile along the wide Culham Reach, sometimes called the Regatta Reach, which is excellent for dinghy sailing. As we bear left towards Abingdon, we pass on the right the entrance to the old, disused SWIFT DITCH spanned by a towpath footbridge of timber. The Ditch by-passes the town and creates Andersey Island. It is probably the original stream of the river. About a hundred yards beyond the footbridge across a pool stands the old stone structure of Culham, or Culhamford, Bridge, built in 1416 according to Leland, who describes it as a 'very fair Bridge of 7 Arches'. Now this beautiful old structure with its pointed arches is burdened by two unsightly concrete gun posts which, no doubt, will stand until the Day of Doom.

Of the Swift Ditch Thacker writes: 'This now almost unknown feature of Thames topography possesses an important and extremely interesting history'. He summarises it thus: (1) To begin with the Ditch contained the whole of the river's water. (2) The monks of Abingdon cut a trench between 936 and 955 A.D. which is still called the Abbey Millstream. (3) The present navigation was cut in 1060. (4) The Swift Ditch was re-opened by the Oxford-Burcot Commission in 1624 when the Abingdon route had, perhaps, become too shallow. (5) The present channel was reopened in 1790 and the Swift Ditch was again abandoned.

'I visited the ancient pathetic scene twice in the summer of 1910', writes Thacker about the Swift Ditch in his *Thames Highway:*

I walked and scrambled, trespassing as 'I piously believe', beside the lonely, grown up watercourse, down as far as the halfway bridge; and there beheld on the left bank the foundation stones on which the weir beam formerly reposed. It was a revelation of much Thames beauty almost undreamed of: lying unvisited and unknown under the grassy slopes of the little ridge . . . For the most part the course was winding and narrow; thickly grown up and overhung with a jungle of plants and hedges and lofty timber that almost shut out the sunlight from its quiet flow.

The foundation stones to which Thacker refers must be those built by the Oxford-Burcot Commission.

ANDERSEY ISLAND is still free of buildings. May it always remain so, for its meadows form a verdant contrast to the tightly built-up town of ABINGDON on the opposite bank. The approach to Abingdon is marred by some dull municipal housing which ignores the river and is without character—a perfect example of how the river banks should not be treated. The Army added a mess of concrete hazards which were still there in 1951 and the electrical engineers have erected a mad jumble of posts and overhead wires.

Once past this unsightliness, however, old Abingdon greets us with charming courtesy. This is indeed a lovely town, the Queen of the Thames—and she is especially lovely when seen from the river or from Andersey Island. From wherever you look a beautifully coloured Dutch picture is composed. Old, warm and weathered bricks and tiles stand there dominated by the soaring stone spire of St. Helen's Church, a rare spire with its flying buttresses and one of John Masefield's three—

> Gleaming with swinging wind-cocks on their perches . . .
> And three giant glares making the heavens dun,
> Oxford and Wallingford and Abingdon.

There is much to see in the town. First is the ancient stone bridge thoroughly restored in the 1920s, though it goes back with Culham Bridge to 1416. For building it Leland says 'every Man had a Penny a Day, which was the best wages, and an Extraordinary Price in those times.' He also notes that 'the great Stone Bridge at Abendun, made by John of St. Hellen, was a great decay to Walyngford, for that the Glosceashire men had usyd Walyngford, that now go by Abyndun. Of aunceient tyme ther was no Bridge at Abbandune, but a Ferie.' Leland is wrong there for there is evidence that a bridge did exist at Abingdon before 1416—probably made of wood.

Ahead across the bridge rises a great, grey building with a star plan, stern but dignified. It is the old prison built in 1801, now used as a granary and one day, if the plans mature, to be the local repertory theatre.

On the right, as you enter the town from the bridge, stand the remains of the great Abbey. This was founded in the year 675 by Cissa, a king of the West Saxons; it suffered in the Danish invasions, became the residence for a while of William the Conqueror and the school of his son Henry, who received here the name Beauclerc, the good student, and then it grew into one of the most splendid of monastic establishments in Europe. The power and confidence of the Abbots resulted in frequent quarrels between the monks and the local people, many of whom had themselves grown wealthy through the local cloth trade. The Abbot owned the privilege of holding a full market in the town and this stirred up rivalry and jealousy in the folk of Oxford and Wallingford as well. By 1327 feelings were running so high that a great riot was organized against the Abbey by the leading men of Oxford and the citizens of Abingdon. The Abbey was sacked and a great part of its buildings were burned to the ground. Nevertheless, in spite of such local dissension, the place flourished right up to the Dissolution in 1538, when it was the first of the more important monasteries to make a voluntary surrender to the King. Evidence shows that at one time the abbey buildings with its gardens and vineyards covered an area of at least three miles in circumference. Today all that is left is the 15th-century gate near the market place, a guest house with a timber gallery on its first floor of the same period, and the 13th-century prior's house with its so-called Checker (Exchequer or Counting House) and its vaulted crypt. This Checker is interesting on account of its great fireplace with stone canopy and its unique gabled chimney with side vents in the form of triple lancets. Fragments from the abbey survive among the winding paths and rockeries in the gardens of the big house near by where they were set up during the last century as decorative sham ruins.

The town contains two parish churches. St. Nicholas, adjoining the Abbey Gate House, was built in the 12th century and was formerly used by the lay servants of the abbey. It is remarkable for its curious stone lantern niche with smoke funnel, its Jacobean pulpit and its tomb with effigies of John and Jane Blacknall who both died on the same day in 1625.

St. Helen's Church, whose noble Perpendicular spire is the district's dominating landmark, is the more interesting. It lies on the far side of the town and is approached by the winding medieval street of East St. Helen's—a superb piece of pictorial townscape. The church is exceptional in possessing no less than five naves. These are all late Gothic, the southern one being as late as 1539, and they create an unusual church plan in that the width is as great as the length—the natural result of a constricted site. Inside are many good monuments and details including a Jacobean pulpit, a striking monument by John Hickey to the Hawkins family of 1780 ('crowded', according to Dickens, 'with busts of fat naked children weeping tears of colossal size') and the altar tomb of John Roysse, gent, who founded the local Grammar School and died in 1571. It is typical of his age that this foundation, having been established in the 63rd year of his life and in the 63rd year of the century, should have been set up to educate 63 boys.

The finest thing in the church by far is the ceiling of the Lady Chapel. It consists of elaborate wood carving framing brilliantly coloured biblical figures painted on wood panels— mostly kings and prophets of the Tree of Jesse. This is a rare, if not unique, English example of late 14th-century artistry, a treasure of national importance. It was properly cleaned in 1935 and a year afterwards the late Dr. Tancred Borenius, famous art historian, wrote in the *Burlington Magazine*.

From whatever point of view we regard it, the recovery of the Tree of Jesse at Abingdon must be classed amongst the most notable additions to the existing material which have ever taken place in the domain of English Medieval painting. No future study of the latter subject can henceforth afford to ignore this magnificent example of painted ceiling decoration in England during the reign of Richard II, all the more so as it also has important bearings on international aspects of the history of art in this period.

To the west of the church cluster three blocks of ancient almshouses. The oldest is that of the Long Alley Almshouses built in 1446 by the Guild of the Holy Cross, a kind of local mutual aid society who had constructed the bridges at Culham and Abingdon. It is a building of some character with a long covered way giving access to the rooms and running the entire length. This ambulatory is screened by an arcading of carved oak above which runs a wide coved cornice. At the centre is a porch of 1625 giving entrance to a communal hall with Jacobean furniture and panelling which is surmounted by a lantern of the early 17th century (the date 1707 upon it merely indicates a time of repair). The other side of the building faces a garden and is surmounted by an impressive and rhythmical row of tall chimneys.

As the Guild grew in strength, funds flowed in and one of its duties became to make provision for 'thirteen poor sick and impotent men and women'—a duty which the Long Alley Almshouses fulfilled. The fraternity, which has an interesting history, brought much benefit besides this to the town. By the second half of the 15th century it was at its zenith and had by then come to act as the representative of the citizens mainly as a counterweight to the dominating influence of the Abbey. But after the Dissolution this guild, as well as the other Abingdon guild, that of Our Lady, which was responsible for the fine church ceiling just described, was suppressed and its funds were swept into the coffers of Edward VI. In 1553 Christ's Hospital was formed to administer the old almshouses and increase relief of the poor.

On the south of the churchyard stand the Brick Alley Alms-houses of a pleasing Dutch-Wrennish brick character erected in 1720 to house eighteen inmates. You can see the end gable of the Long Alley building from the river and just above it the full façade of Brick Alley. In 1859 these houses were merged into the Christ's Hospital Foundation.

To the north of the churchyard are Twitty's Almshouses, another charming brick building with classical details, which were founded by Charles Twitty, a native of the town, in 1706. These are independent of Christ's Hospital and house three men and three women. Abingdon contains other almshouses, notably those of Tompkins in Ock Street built round a court-yard in 1733.

Ock Street is long, wide and straight in contrast to the other narrow, winding thoroughfares of the town. It contains a number of good Georgian houses and several old inns with in-teresting signs. Note especially that of the beflagged *Air Balloon* and the humorous *Mr. Warwick's Arms*. In Ock Street also is an austere but dignified Baptist Chapel with Tuscan columns of 1841.

An important and dominating building in Abingdon is the stone County Hall in the Market Place built in 1677-83 by Christopher Kempster, one of Wren's master masons at St. Paul's Cathedral. It is possible that Wren himself had a hand in the design for it is a stately building which bears his stamp. It has an arcaded market place below and a hall above which is faced outside with pilasters, the whole being surmounted by a lantern. The chamber is now a local museum containing such diverse objects as fossils and a Victorian doll's house.

Other sights in the town are the several fine houses of the 17th and 18th centuries in West St. Helen's Street and else-where. In fact, wherever you go in Abingdon you will find some building or some architectural detail that is worth more than a glance. May the *Friends of Abingdon* fight sturdily for their preservation.

The three miles above ABINGDON LOCK make a fine reach,

largely on account of the grounds of NUNEHAM PARK which
rise from the river on the Oxfordshire side. The only jarring
note is the railway bridge, known as Black Bridge. It has been
wisely said that it is best to see Nuneham Reach from this
bridge because from any other point it is necessary to see the
bridge itself. Beyond this eyesore we pass an island on the right
where a rustic foot bridge and a decaying thatched cottage
called Lock Cottage (for there was a lock here once) provide a
piece of Victorian decoration. You dare not land here now for
fear of trespassing but sixty years ago, when the river was better
appreciated, this was a gay public spot. D. S. MacColl writing
at that time says:

> Presently one comes upon a little island connected with the Nuneham side by
> an intensely rustic bridge. By the landing-place is a cottage with exaggerated
> thatch. Here they make tea. They make most not for the University picnics that
> the summer term brings to these hospitable woods, but when the revolt of the town
> sets in with the long vacation. The river is as populous as ever then with dashing
> young fellows in flannel, and enchanting young ladies dressed in the depth of
> fashion. Great and many barges are towed down to Nuneham, and there merry
> people dance round Carfax, and float up again to Salter's in the heavy purple
> dusk, trolling snatches of song.

In these democratic days our despotism is less benevolent.
Nuneham was sold to Oxford University in 1947 and it is now
occupied by the R.A.F. whose object in life is not to purvey
pleasure.

The Carfax to which MacColl refers is an interesting piece of
decorative stonework which can be seen up on the hill just beyond the island. It looks like a monument of some sort but it is
in fact the old conduit head displaced from Carfax, Oxford.
When the High was widened in 1787 and this redundant conduit head became a nuisance to the coaches, it was presented
to the Earl of Harcourt who had it set up here in his park. It
was built in 1610 by Otho Nicholson, whose initials are carved
on the structure, its purpose being to supply the city with pure
water brought from a hill above North Hinksey. It is an attractive, elaborate affair, carved in the Jacobean manner with mermaids, dragons, unicorns and other devices; the Empress Maud
is there, too, riding an Ox over a Ford above the cistern. This
is an unusual kind of park decoration for the period when it
was set up, for then follies and sham Gothik castle ruins were

all the vogue. Before the presentation, a castle had in fact been projected for the site on which the conduit stands.

The estate here originally belonged to the Courtenay family but in 1710 Simon, Viscount Harcourt, then Lord Chancellor (a successful lawyer who had won the celebrated Sacheverell Case and had prosecuted Defoe), bought the property when it contained only a small old manor. He did nothing to the place and it was his grandson who built the Palladian mansion we now see. His architect was S. Leadbetter, who designed the Radcliffe Infirmary in Oxford, and the house was completed in about 1760, much of the stone coming from the demolished Stanton Harcourt house, the family's former seat. The building does not seem to have much to say for itself but the setting is very fine. As that lover of elegance and comfort, Horace Walpole, remarked after his first visit to Nuneham in 1773: 'Nuneham astonished me with the first *coup d'œil* of its ugliness, and the next day it charmed me. It is as rough as a bear, but capable of being made a most agreeable scene . . . Nuneham is not superb, but so calm, *riant* and comfortable, so live-at-able; one wakes in the morning on a whole picture of beauty.' This description may give the reason why Queen Victoria decided to spend her honeymoon here.

The grounds, laid out by 'Capability' Brown, are superb. As an article in *Country Life* aptly described them, they consist 'in a wide amphitheatre of stately trees, with the house, as it were, in the centre of the dress-circle, and the river the orchestra.' They typify a style of landscaping which is peculiarly English and which the whole world has acknowledged to be unsurpassed—the informal, picturesque park whose inspiration came from such painters as Claude and Poussin. Brown, the man who could see 'capability of much improvement' and among other work laid out many gardens in the Thames Valley including Blenheim, was its most enthusiastic and successful developer. Apart from laying out the grounds he did a little building at Nuneham at a time when he was in partnership with Henry Holland, for in 1780 he added the wings.

An interesting little building, lying near the house, but which is hidden by trees from the river is the church of 1764, with a squat dome and Doric portico, designed by James 'Athenian' Stuart. Originally this was the village church but became the domestic chapel when a new church was built nearer the village in 1880.

NUNEHAM COURTENAY VILLAGE is a curiosity. The building of the great house involved the demolition, not only of the old manor, but the ruthless removal of a whole village as well. A new model village was then built for the evacuees on the main coaching road to the north-east of the estate. It is pleasant enough and consists of simple blocks of standardized brick cottages lining a half mile of road behind rows of great elm trees. One might call it a New Village of the 18th century, for, with Milton Abbas, it is one of the first examples of deliberate village planning and complete reconstruction for a community by one landlord.

Facing the northern boundary of Nuneham Park across the river is Radley College boathouse. Near this spot Colonel Harcourt proposed to the Conservators in 1889 that a bridge should be built. It was to be little more than a way for cattle. Construction did actually begin but the project was discontinued in 1892 and a ferry was established here instead.

LOWER RADLEY is composed of scattered thatched cottages in strong contrast to UPPER RADLEY with its dull modern villas. If it were not for the church we should not visit it, but the church must be seen because its interior is rich in fine things. First, there is the unusual coloured monument to Sir William Stonhouse and family of 1631 with its figure of a bearded soldier who kneels and prays over two recumbent bodies. Next, there is the pulpit canopy from the old House of Commons presented to the church by Speaker Lenthall in 1653. After that, the 17th-century stalls should be noticed. But the real beauty of the church is in the heraldic windows of the 15th and 16th centuries, which burn in ambers, greens and reds. The designs include the coats of arms of Richard III, Henry VI and Henry VIII while the west window contains a portrait said to be that of Henry VII. The glass was not designed for the church, for which it is, indeed, rather too large in scale. It was presented in 1840 by Thomas Willement, a very good craftsman in stained glass himself, who set these old pieces in the church with some armorial glass of his own.

Beyond the church is Radley House which became the famous public school in 1847—a brick building begun in 1727 and added to later in the century.

Two miles above Nuneham we reach SANDFORD LOCK, the deepest on the river. which is dominated on the right by a paper mill and chimney. The mill is 19th-century but stands on the site of one built by the Knights Templar in the late 13th century. Here one of the three earliest pound locks on the Thames was built in the 17th century by the Oxford-Burcot Commission. Let us now walk up past the *King's Arms* to the small church. Though of no particular interest in itself it contains an extremely beautiful piece of alabaster carving—one of the riverside treasures. Unfortunately it has been hung high up in a dark corner on the south of the chancel and deserves to be better placed and lit. It represents the Assumption of the Virgin who is upheld by angels and it has a reliquary at the base on which can be seen traces of gilding and colour. Found buried for preservation in the church porch, it came probably either from the chapel of the Knights Hospitaller of St. John or of the Benedictine Nunnery, both of which lay in the parish in medieval times, and both of which possessed chapels dedicated to the Virgin.

From Sandford to Oxford we sense, rather than see, the nearness of industrialism and close building, and even here the river retains much of its verdant character. The next point of interest is IFFLEY, a village still unspoiled in spite of the encroachments of Oxford. It contains, for your pleasure, a tea house and garden by the side of the mill stream. The tea house, aptly named Grist Cottage, was indeed once part of the famous mill which was burned down in 1908. The main feature of the village, however, is the church, remarkable as one of the most complete Norman churches in England, being built mainly between 1175 and 1182 without transepts, aisles or chapels and with round arches highly decorated with zig-zags, beak mouldings, grotesques, centaurs and mounted knights in battle. The church has a contemporary font of black marble for complete infant immersion. Take special note here of the west and south doors.

A modern concrete footbridge makes an entrance arch to the Oxford reach. This is a graceful structure showing that modern materials and ways of building need not be out of key with the river style. Only the fussy 'architectural' handrails mar an otherwise excellent piece of engineering design. A short distance beyond the bridge on the left is the municipal bathing place partly hidden with typical burgher puritanism behind an unsightly fence. About a quarter of a mile further on we pass, on the same side, the University Boat House and, on the facing side, just beyond the entrance to the Cherwell, the row of COLLEGE BARGES along the edge of Christ Church Meadow begins.

These barges have an interesting history. The Oxford undergraduates did not discover the river as a sporting resort until the 1830s. The discovery occurred when some physical outlet was needed to take the place of such activities as bell ringing which had gone out of fashion. It resulted in the formation in 1839 of the University Boat Club and the institution of that bumping system of racing which the narrowness of the river compels. The main racing of the year takes place during Eights Week which is the equivalent of Cambridge's May Week (so-called because it comes in June and lasts a fortnight). Then these college barges come into their own as grandstands from which to watch the finish of the races.

Colleges began to acquire the ornate procession barges discarded by the City Livery Companies as floating club houses when interest in the new pastime began to grow, but the only original City Barge still remaining, and the best in appearance, is that of Oriel College which can be recognised by its row of oval windows, carved angels and long, graceful prow. The others were specially built for the colleges in Victorian and Edwardian times, many being designed by architects, each battling for his pet style with colourful panache. Unhappily, just before the war a few colleges gave up their barges and erected for themselves those brick buildings you can see on the bank opposite the University Boat House. No doubt they are very convenient, and are served with hot water and shower baths, but how dull they look compared with the barges, how clearly they symbolise this stern, humourless, futilitarian age. The war saved the barges, for the time being at least, and one can but hope that the colleges will now set to work to preserve them for good, and—why not —install in them some plumbing and other useful things, for these fantastic structures are as much a part of Oxford as Tom Tower and Magdalen Bridge. 'The oddest little street, this row of motley Noah's Arks', D. S.

MacColl calls them. 'And when the high poles shake out their amazing flags', he continues, 'and the men come down in fearless college colours, and a vast and diverse millinery decks every foot of standing room the roofs can give, there would seem to be some touch of an Arabian Night about a very English day, were it not that the vigorous people wear many more colours than Arabia would allow.'

And here we are at last at Folly Bridge and its lively little shipping pool. OXFORD will, of course, be visited but you will need a whole book on its own to tell you all about that. Here only the things of the river at Oxford will be described.

Carfax Conduit

8

Oxford to the Source

FOLLY BRIDGE WAS BUILT IN 1825 and must look very different from its predecessor, the old Grand Pont of the Norman builders with its eighteen arches and its strange tower. This tower was at first probably a defensive work but became the study of Friar Bacon, the medieval (and, in his day, highly suspect) scientist and astronomer, 'whose wonderful proficiency in natural philosophy had obtained for him the reputation of a necromancer', as an 18th-century writer describes him. Until his death in Oxford in 1294, Bacon seems to have used this tower as an observatory as well as a study. Much later a citizen called Welcome repaired the study and added another storey which became known as Welcome's Folly. Hence the name of the present bridge. The tower was demolished in 1779, sold standing for £13.

More or less on the same spot as this tower, now rises a strange house, also something of a folly. It was built by a moneylender in 1849 in a queer, indeterminate style, being decorated with terra-cotta statues in niches and having something of Venice about it. It is no great work of art but it is amusing and suggests that whoever designed it did, at least, enjoy himself.

Just below the bridge on the Berkshire side, doubled by its reflection in the backwater, stands a much more dignified dwelling, a Georgian mansion called GRAND PONT HOUSE, which can be seen best from the towpath footbridge. On the other side of the river here a small brook comes into the river called the TRILL MILL STREAM. This runs along to decorate the War Memorial Garden of Christ Church and then, turning north-east, disappears underground for half a mile when it joins the old river channel near Abbey Place. At one time the

Friar Bacon's Study

stream was open and, running as a mill stream through gardens
(now a drab built-up area), it formed, with the river, an island
on which stood two great religious houses, one Dominican, the
other Franciscan, now perpetuated only in place names such
as Friars Street, Blackfriars Road and Preachers' Pool. In the
Thames Magazine, Mr. Alan Smith has described how, as a
youth, he made an adventurous journey by canoe down this
underground waterway with two companions. One of them
was an unknown schoolboy at Oxford High School. He is dead
now but he will be remembered for a very long time by the
whole world as Lawrence of Arabia.

Keep right at Folly Bridge, because the branch to the left,
which once contained a lock, is rather narrow. Now we must
bear with a mile of squalor—of gasworks, railway sidings and
semi-slumdom. But even here are some things worth looking
at—for instance, the Regency house on the right with its grace-
fully detailed iron verandah. The house is topped by the un-
couth gasholders, but these, too, can sometimes be impressive
when the sun strikes them from the right direction to cast
intricate patterns of latticework, curved and fretted, onto the
great cylinders. Neither are the industrial buildings by the
water beyond Osney Lock altogether displeasing: they produce
a quiet, canal-like impression.

Mind your head at OSNEY BRIDGE, which was built much

too low in 1889, the distance between the top of the arch and the water at standard summer level being only 7 feet, 7 inches. We are now not on the original river navigation, which runs further east past the Castle and under Hythe Bridge; we are on the so-called Weir Stream, the present main navigation. This is believed to be a cut engineered by the monks of Osney Abbey to obtain a flow of water for their mill.

Of the magnificent abbey, which once stood near Osney Bridge, not a stone can be seen, though some ruins remained at least up to the 18th century when Dr. Johnson gazed upon them with such indignation. At the Dissolution Wolsey appropriated the abbey's wealth and materials for his new foundation of Christ Church. Great Tom, the curfew bell of Oxford, once hung in the tall belfry of the abbey. Nothing is left, either, of Rewley Abbey (from *roy lieu*) which occupied the northern end of Osney Island.

At FIDDLERS ISLAND the river puts on her green party dress again. Ahead, gracing the river like a necklace, a white-painted iron footbridge carries the towpath in a graceful curve across to the island. It is a simple lattice structure, another good example of how well the engineers design when they do not try to be architects—even as long ago as 1865, the year the bridge was built. Just by the bridge on the left is MEDLEY MANOR, at one time an oratory attached to Godstow Nunnery—a farm before the Conquest and a farm today.

Beyond Fiddlers Island on the right, the wide, breezy expanse of PORT MEADOW opens out, 439 acres in extent, the property today of the Freemen of Oxford as it has been since the time of Edward the Confessor, where every burgher still has the right of pasturage. Opposite is BINSEY (*Benea ea*, the Island of Prayer), the only Oxfordshire Parish on the Berkshire bank. It has only an inn and a few houses but we should land here to take a half-mile walk to the church, a very pleasant walk, the last part of which runs down an avenue of trees. The church is old and still lit by oil lamps, but the most interesting object here lies on the west of the church in the churchyard. It is the little HOLY WELL OF ST. MARGARET, miraculously opened by the sainted virgin Frideswide after she had built here in 730 a chapel of 'wallyns and rough-hewn timber'. A stream of pilgrims thereafter resorted to the well, for its waters were believed to have magic healing properties. As a result a large town of 65,000 inhabitants grew up near-by called Seckworth, containing no less than eleven churches, twenty-four inns and many dwellings for the priests required to confess and absolve the many penitent travellers. In 1158 the saint's shrine and priory were moved to Oxford and soon Seckworth dwindled and finally vanished away.

At GODSTOW LOCK turn round for a moment to see the distant spires of Oxford pricking the sky across Port Meadow, and, once through the lock, look left to see the remains of GODSTOW NUNNERY. They are few enough—a precinct wall and the skeleton of a small chapel. The Nunnery was consecrated in 1138, being founded in this delectable spot by a matron named Editha who then presided here as abbess over twenty-four nuns. The place is, of course, famed for its connection with the fair Rosamund de Clifford, who became leman of Henry II. Here she was educated and subsequently buried. Her romantic story has become a legend and, to use Ireland's words, 'as the mind is naturally fond of incident bordering on romance, this legendary tale, as it beguiles the moment, may plead an apology for its introduction.'

It seems that the King, 'a man of low stature and fat of body, of a fresh colour, and of good expression in his speech', noticed Rosamund one day near the nunnery when she was already famed for her wit and beauty, 'became enamoured, declared his passion and triumphed over her honour.' He removed her to his palace at Woodstock close by, where he secreted her in a bower protected by a maze of arches and winding walls of stone. Here she remained several years, frequently visited by the king, whose ardour was increased rather than cloyed by enjoyment. But one day his jealous queen discovered the way through the maze, some say by an unravelled ball of silk dropped by Rosamund, and presented a cup of poison to her rival. Historians dispute this but most agree that she died soon after her concealment in the bower and that her body was then interred in the choir of Godstow Nunnery within a sumptuous and wonderfully contrived tomb. The Bishop of Lincoln on a visit discovered this tomb covered in silk and lit by many tapers. In sudden zeal he cried out: 'Take the Harlot from hence and bury her without the church.' But Rosamund had been popular, even among the womenfolk, and, after all, a king has privileges. The body was removed only to the chapter house, where, says Speed, 'the chaste sisters gathered her bones, and put them in a perfumed bag, inclosing them so in a lead, and layde them againe in the church under a fayre large grave-stone.' Leland records that after the dissolution of the nunnery, 'Rosamunde's tumbe at Godstowe nunnery was taken up of late; it is a stone with this inscription, 'Tumba Rosamundae'; her bones were closed in lede, and within that, bones were closed in lether; when it was opened, there was a sweet smell came out of it.' And now:

> The wind-flower waves, in lonely bloom,
>   On Godstow's desolated wall:
> There thin shades flit through twilight gloom,
>   And murmured accents feebly fall.
> The aged hazel nurtures there
> Its hollow fruit, so seeming fair,
> And lightly throws its humble shade,
> Where Rosamonda's form is laid.'

So wrote Thomas Love Peacock in his poem *The Genius of the Thames*, first published in 1810, inspired perhaps by pleasant river excursions made with his pale friend Shelley, who also wrote of the Thames and resided for a while by its side at Marlow.

Across the bridge from the nunnery lies the well-known resort of undergraduates, the TROUT INN, once the guest house of the nunnery. This is a lovely spot, with a generous terrace looking across the weir stream to an island garden where a stone lion, which once decorated the gates of Tusmore Park, rears its crowned head above the briars. In the other direction, westward, the road takes you to the village of WYTHAM, a picturesque place of thatch and limestone cottages set among magnificent woods. The so-called Abbey here, until recently the seats of the Abingdons but now owned by Oxford University, was built in Tudor times and, though much altered since, retains its gate-house and hall. The church, which was rebuilt in 1814 with materials taken from Cumnor Place, contains a good east window holding some 17th-century Flemish glass in blues and yellows; also some small but good pieces of armorial glass in other windows, and an intriguing grotesque corbel of a bagpipe player.

Here at Wytham the author trespassed one day into a large, unkempt yard where the outhouses were tumbling down and a sad-looking dog-cart stood deep and immovable among the weeds. A country labourer came hobbling through a break in the brick wall. He was old and solemn. When asked what the place was, he replied:

' 'Tis the work-yard of the big house. Just look at it. Why, I remember the time when it were full of men and busy enough. Over there was the wood-cutter's store and next to it the brick-layer's stocks. That there (indicating with his stick a pile of rubble crowned with loosestrife) was the carpenter's shop—all for keepin' up the estate. Fifteen gardeners they had up there then. Now there's two.'

How did he find living now compared with the old days when he was young? He shook his head slowly.

' 'Twas far better then. Times was better for rich *and* poor. We didn't get much pay but we lived well, and food was good and plenty of it. Now after you've eaten you start rumblin' again in an hour and the food don't taste of nothin'. The beer was better in the old days too. Today you don't know what you're eatin' and drinkin'. An' why don't you ever see a 'op afloat in a tankard, like you used to?'

That was an old countryman's attitude, and it is probably true to say that whereas life in the towns may have improved for the majority in a great many ways, in the country it has lost much of its old *Tom Jones* savour. Certainly this ruined work-yard was no symbol of good living. The old man had the right sense of values and if he had been born three generations earlier would have firmly supported William Cobbett, who held among so many other sensible notions: 'Good eating, good drinking, good lodging; without these people do not really live; it is stay-ing upon the earth.' Today we have cheap entertainment, we are all washed, our kippers come wrapped in cellophane, marg-arine is mistaken for butter, but we seem to have lost even our desire for the three basic good things.

From Godstow the Thames suddenly changes its character. It grows narrower, it twists surprisingly, and, until Lechlade, no town or even village touches the banks. We shall have to walk a mile or two to the villages to do our shopping and see the sights. This is the medieval Thames, quiet and changeless. For the first few miles the landscape is at its loveliest with WYTHAM HILL and Woods rising from the Berkshire side and the ancient spire of Cassington Church forming a landmark above the Oxfordshire willows ahead. Wytham Hill is 539 feet high and bears the mound of a castle built by Kinewulf, King of the West Saxons, when he was fighting the Mercian King Offa.

The last time the author passed through KING'S LOCK, Mr. Fred Smith was its keeper. There was little traffic and time to chat, to learn something maybe of a lock-keeper's life. The river ran in Fred's blood. For at least three hundred years back his forebears had been watermen and he had himself served as a registered lighterman on the lower river. He proudly displayed his apprenticeship indenture, worn and stained, for it had been with him five times under water. It contained this curious, archaic wording:

WATERMENS COMPANY. 1514-1859. This Indenture Witnesseth, That Frederick Smith, Son of John Lowden Smith of the Parish of Rotherhithe in the County of London doth put himself Apprentice to John Lowden Smith (aforesaid) of the Parish Aforesaid in the County Aforesaid, a Freeman of the Company of Watermen and Lightermen of the River Thames—to learn his Art, and with him (after the manner of an Apprentice) to dwell and serve upon the River of Thames from the Day of the Date hereof until the full End and Term of five years from thence next following, to be fully complete and ended: during which Term the said Apprentice his said Master faithfully shall serve as aforesaid, his Secrets keep, his lawful Commandments everywhere gladly do; . . . He shall not commit Fornication nor contract Matrimony within the said Term; He shall not play at Cards, Dice, Tables, nor any other unlawful games whereby his said Master may have any loss . . . He shall not haunt Taverns, nor Play-Houses, nor absent himself from his Master's Service Day nor Night, unlawfully . . .

—and so on. In return the said Master

shall teach and instruct, or cause to be taught and instructed, finding unto the said Apprentice Meat, Drink, Apparel, Lodging, and all other Necessaries according to the Custom of the City of London.

Fred recounted many of the adventures he had experienced in the tough, vigorous life of the London docks to which his present, quiet days were so great a contrast. But he seemed to be enjoying his present days and it is clear that there must be many worse occupations than that of lock-keeping on the

Thames. The life is healthy, and though it gives fairly hard work in the summer, in the winter there is time enough to develop one's personal interests, for one is off duty by sundown. A well-built cottage and an adequate garden are provided free; one is king in one's own small terrain which is surrounded by the friendly English countryside; there are always new faces to see and new friends to be made. The pay varies with the size and traffic of the lock and tends to diminish the higher upstream one goes. It is not excessive but one can augment income by sidelines such as running a tea-garden, selling garden produce or following some spare-time craft such as the making of boating or fishing accessories. For a nature lover, a poet, or a philosopher, fond of quiet and simple things, could there be a better way of living than to be a lock-keeper on the Upper Thames?

Lock-keepers, however, are rarely poets, and, before the war at least, were mostly pensioned petty officers of the Navy—a fine type who kept the locks beautifully trim. In these days of labour shortage recruiting is wider but preference is usually given to men with some understanding of the whims of water. The strange thing about these men is that, although they may grumble as much as any of us, they rarely leave the work, and, if they do, sooner or later return to it. One old lock-keeper told the author that he had at one time given up his job for a much better paid position away from the river. Within three months he was back.

'I don't know why it was', he said, 'but I just felt miserable away from the water. Perhaps it's that fine feeling you get of being able to control something bigger and more powerful than yourself. It's the same with most of us. When a lock-keeper retires you'd think he had had enough of water. Not a bit of it. The old fellow who had my job before he retired, for instance; What does he do when he goes for a walk? Comes straight down here to see what the water's doing and make sure I'm letting enough over the weir.'

Just beyond King's Lock on the right the DUKE'S CUT (owned by the Duke of Marlborough) joins the river and gives a weedy access to the OXFORD CANAL about half a mile to the east. Once on the Oxford Canal the whole waterway system of England would lie before us, a little known but fascinating world, as the author himself discovered when he ventured off the Thames just here in 1948 to make a six-hundred-mile exploration up to Llangollen and eventually back down the Grand Union to join the Thames again at Brentford.*

Soon the Evenlode flows into the river on our right and a short way beyond it can be seen another weedy entrance. This is the old, disused Cassington Canal which joins the Evenlode three miles up. Another mile along this peaceful reach brings us to EYNSHAM LOCK and the noble SWINFORD BRIDGE. This bridge was built in 1777 by the Earl of Abingdon, 'whose liberality and public spirit', as a contemporary notes, 'have, I am credibly informed, been amply repaid by the revenue derived from this undertaking'. In 1950 it was still a toll bridge where a penny a wheel was charged. With its subtly curving sweep, its diminishing arches, careful classical detailing and satisfying stone texture, it is perhaps the finest of the many fine bridges of the river. On the Berkshire side here rises BEACON HILL, bearing the signs of an early British camp. On this hill, it is said, one of the beacons blazed out the signal that the Spanish Armada was approaching our shores. Below the hill, near the river, a large brick building, housing the local water works disrupts the scene. Better by far would have been a direct, engineering approach to its design, however unsightly the result, than this Georgian 'architecture'.

EYNSHAM lies a mile distant on the Oxfordshire side, a place famous long ago for its magnificent Benedictine Abbey, of which all that now remains is a window in the vicarage garden. The little town itself is picturesque with its Cotswold stone cottages, its market square and late-Gothic church, but has nothing exceptional to show you apart from a very old and dilapidated market cross. As at Goring you can here buy your bread, warm and savoury, straight from the oven.

A mile on is trim PINKHILL LOCK and three miles beyond, through unexciting scenery, we reach famous BABLOCK HYTHE in Scholar Gypsy land. Bab-lock-Hythe: three dull syllables which together make poetry. The lyricism of this spot is today marred somewhat by a modern inn with green tiles on the roof and horizontal glazing bars in the windows. In the

* See *The Canals of England* by Eric de Maré: Architectural Press.

meadow nearby a row of railway carriages arc laid out to form a miniature holiday camp, but thanks to bright paint-work, some bunting and a screen of trees, the effect does not insult the landscape half as much as the inn. Ahead on the opposite bank lie other strange dwellings in the shape of double-decker buses. This kind of thing usually brings out-bursts of abuse from all except the owners of such extemporary homes, but usually for the wrong reasons. They are associated in our minds with poverty and squalor, but there is, after all, no intrinsic reason why tramcars, buses or railway carriages should not be made into attractive structures if treated with gaiety, feeling and an Emett-like fantasy. Let us adopt a toler-ant, hopeful attitude, then, to the individualists who enjoy the river at Bablock Hythe.

A large car ferry crosses the river here, worked with a chain and a wheel, descendant of a line of ferries which have plied at this crossing since the 13th century. In proof of this, a refer-ence of 1279 notes 'the ferry of Babbelak', while a manuscript of 1692 states that 'Bablock Hythe has a great boat to carry over Carts and Coaches.'

While here, let us stroll up the field path for a mile or so to CUMNOR, in the direction of Matthew Arnold's 'warm, green-muffled Cumnor Hills'. Cumnor is a pleasant Berkshire village to which the Abbots of Abingdon would retire when they were sick, but it is better known through Sir Walter Scott's *Kenil-worth*, a historical romance which seems to have little basis in fact. Its main object of interest today is the spiral staircase of oak leading to the belfry in the tower of the church. It is proudly signed 'TB GN 1685'—a superb piece of craftsman-ship and a considerable structural feat for the time it was built, being supported entirely by its central post.

Other interesting sights in the church include a manorial pew, chancel rails and pulpit of Jacobean period, two Eliza-bethan brasses, a chained *Bible* of 1611 and a statue of Queen Elizabeth, said to have been sculptured for the Earl of Leicester and erected here in 1888 after it had been discovered in an out-house of Wytham Abbey. Here also is the 16th-century tomb of Sir Anthony Forster, whom Scott supposed to have murdered Amy Robsart at the instigation of her husband, Lord Dudley, and of Queen Elizabeth. It seems that the only evidence in favour of the theory is that the lady's death would have made possible a marriage between Queen Elizabeth and Lord Dudley, who became the Earl of Leicester. At Cumnor is recorded the last act of public penance which took place here in 1748: the penitent was required to appear, 'On Sunday during Morning Prayer' wearing 'a large white sheet from shoulders to ankles, white rod in hand, bare-legged, bare-footed, open-faced in the middle of the aisle or passage of this same church that she may be well seen and heard.'

Two miles from Bablock Hythe on the Oxfordshire side lies the fascinating village of STANTON HARCOURT which must be visited. Near the village is an airfield from which Mr. Churchill flew in great secrecy to the Yalta Conference. Below this airfield lie three great monoliths, the largest being nine feet high and six feet wide. They are known as the Devil's Quoits and may be either the relics commemorating a fight between Britons and Saxons here in 614, or, more probably, the remains of a Druids' Circle. The local people believed for many centuries, however, that they had been hurled here by the Devil from Cumnor Hills three miles away in a wager for the soul of a man. It is possible that the name Stanton derives from these stones for the Saxon *Stan-tun* means a stone enclosure, a supposition which supports the Druidical theory.

From the 12th century until 1710, the Harcourts were lords of the manor here. Most of their original house has disappeared but Pope's Tower, of the Perpendicular Gothic period, remains. It can easily be mistaken for the church tower and is indeed ecclesiastical, for it originally contained the Harcourts' private chapel with priest's rooms above. To this building Alexander Pope retired for two summers after the family had departed, and here in 1718 he completed his translation of the Fifth Book of Homer. Near the tower is another part of the original house still standing, a curious building with a pyramid roof surmounted by a vane in the form of a griffon, the Harcourt emblem. This was the great kitchen of the house. As Dr. Plot remarks: 'It is so strangely unusual that, by way of riddle, one may truly call it either a kitchen within a chimney or a kitchen without one, for below it is nothing but a large square, and octagonal above, ascending like a tower, the fires being made against the walls, and the smoke climbing up them without any tunnels or disturbance to the cooks, which, being stopped by a large conical roof at the top, goes out at loopholes on every side, according as how the wind sets, the loopholes at the side next the wind being shut by folding doors, and the adverse side open.' It is much like the famous kitchen at Glastonbury.

The church, a mixture of Norman, Early English and Perpendicular, is one of the most beautiful and harmonious in Oxfordshire. In the chancel is the earliest of Early English screens in the country and also a lovely, simple effigy of Maud, wife of Sir Thomas Harcourt, dated 1394. The figure lies in a niche, formerly an Easter Sepulchre which is decorated with a richly carved canopy. On the south lies a chapel containing a number of fine Harcourt tombs, notably that to Sir Robert Harcourt, standard bearer to Henry VII at the Battle of Bosworth, and his Lady Margaret. Both effigies wear the Order of the Garter. On the east wall of this chapel is a large Victorian brass plaque giving the history of this old and distinguished family beginning with one Bernard the Dane who married Sprote de Bourgoyne in 876. Another impressive monument is that containing the busts of Philip Harcourt and his wife, which are surrounded by intricate carving of fine craftsmanship. This is dated 1688, the year James II abdicated in flight.

On the south wall of the church is an epitaph composed by Pope in memory of two country lovers who were killed by lightning. The little, crooked poet was touched by the event and has recorded it in a letter he wrote from his study in the tower to Lady Mary Montagu, then his friend but later to become his hated enemy. 'I have a mind', he writes,

to fill the rest of this paper with an accident that happened just under my eyes, and has made a great impression upon me. I have passed part of this summer at an old romantic seat of my Lord Harcourt's, which he has lent me; it overlooks a common field, where, under the shade of a haycock, sat two lovers, as constant as ever were found in romance, beneath a spreading beech . . . John was a wellset man, about five-and-twenty; Sarah a brown woman of eighteen . . . Their love was the talk, but not the scandal of the neighbourhood, for all they aimed at was the blameless possession of each other in marriage. It was but this very morning that he obtained her parents' consent, and it was but till the next week that they were to wait to be happy. Perhaps this very day, in the intervals of their work, they were talking of their wedding clothes, and John was now matching several kinds of poppies and field-flowers to her complexion, to make her a present of knots for the day. While they were thus employed (it was on the last day of July), a terrible storm of thunder and lightning arose, and drove the labourers to what shelter the trees or hedges afforded. Sarah, frightened and out of breath, sunk on a haycock, and John (who never separated from her) sat by her side, having raked two or three heaps together to secure her. Immediately there was heard so loud a crack as if heaven had burst asunder. The labourers, all solicitous for each other's safety, called to one another; those who were nearest our lovers, hearing no answer, stepped to the place where they lay. They first saw a little smoke, and after, this faithful pair—John with one arm about his Sarah's neck, and the other held over her face, as if to screen her from the lightning. They were dead. There was no mark or discolouring on their bodies, only that Sarah's eyebrow was a little singed, and a small spot between her breasts. They were buried the next day in one grave, in the parish of Stanton Harcourt, in Oxfordshire, where my Lord Harcourt, at my request, has erected a monument over them.

Down the village street, a little way beyond the Manor, stands a fine, if somewhat over-fenestrated, house of stone, built in the 17th century and called Parsonage House. It is now owned by Oxford University and is inhabited, as it deserves to be, by a man of culture and learning. Part of its charm lies in its walled forecourt which, entered by a pair of wrought iron gates, is laid out as a small formal garden giving shelter and privacy amidst the scent of lavender and roses.

NORTHMOOR LOCK, two miles on from Bablock Hythe, is beautifully remote and just above it, on the left, is one of the most delightful moorings of the river. Let us then tie up here and set off to explore two more villages. APPLETON in Berkshire can be reached by an ancient green lane that comes down to the water a hundred yards or so above the weir. The village contains the second of the two oldest inhabited manor houses in Berkshire. This was built mainly in the time of Henry II though parts are even earlier, and it is moated for defence. Held at one time by Thomas Chaucer, son of the poet, it came in 1436 to the Fettiplace family, to one member of which, Sir John, an Elizabethan tomb of 1593 has been erected in the church. In the main street of the village a pair of very old yew trees, carefully clipped with bird forms on top, makes a charming entrance feature to a cottage, while the post office has an entrance porch with a tympanum decorated with naïve, painted plasterwork of the 17th century.

Across the river in Oxfordshire lies NORTHMOOR, whose church bell chimes have come floating to us across the meadows each hour. The cruciform has the customary mixture of Gothic

Above Oxford lies the medieval Thames 'like a stream in a missal'. Here illustrated are three charming bridges of the upper river. ABOVE, the iron lacework of the arc at Fiddlers Island built in 1865. LEFT, Tenfoot Bridge near Buckland, of timber. BELOW, Swinford bridge, built of stone in 1777, perhaps the finest bridge of the Thames; in the distance is the toll house.

LEFT, the cut above Shifford Lock in the evening glow—the most remote spot of the river. BELOW, the 18th-century bridge at Radcot marked for miles around by a pair of giant poplars; near by, over a side stream, stands the oldest bridge of the Thames (page 19).

Down the road from Radcot lies Faringdon in Berkshire. In its old
church kneels, ABOVE, the 17th-century effigy of Dorothy, Lady Unton.
At Kelmscott, BELOW LEFT, is the sturdy manor house where William
Morris and his family lived for many summers—'the type of the pleasant
places of the earth'. BELOW RIGHT, a gravestone of the 18th century in
Buscot churchyard.

At Lechlade we near our journey's end. TOP, the
main street at Lechlade with its 15th-century
church and its 'pratie pyramis of stone'.
ABOVE, Halfpenny Bridge, Lechlade's 18th-cen-
tury toll bridge. LEFT, the medieval carving of
Madonna and Child in Inglesham Church.

styles, though mainly of the 14th century, and is unusual in possessing a 15th-century tower built into the nave. Inside are a number of interesting objects, one being the late 17th-century wooden singers' gallery, also a bell loft, which was used by musicians right up to the end of the 19th century.

In the north transept are two effigies of a Knight Crusader and his lady and also the tomb of Edmund Warcupp, nephew of Speaker Lenthall, dated 1665 and bearing a latin inscription referring to the *Londinium peste* of that year. The end of this tomb bears some excellent stone carving.

Stone carving on Edmund Warcupp's Tomb, Northmoor

To the south of the church stands an Elizabethan house, once the rectory, and near it is a contemporary *columbarium* or dovecote, a type of building now rarely seen but once common enough when dovecotes were not purely decorative adjuncts to the houses but of some economic importance. In the middle of the 17th century England possessed no less than 26,000 of them, but they were doomed when the turnip and the swede were introduced to our agriculture in the early 18th century. This innovation meant that the wholesale slaughter of cattle each autumn was no longer necessary and the breeding of pigeons for fresh winter meat could be dispensed with. The Romans were great breeders of pigeons. The Roman tradition was carried on in France and brought to England at the Conquest. For several centuries the right to build *columbaria* was limited to lords of manors. This was unjust because the pigeon population of England must at one time have consumed at least 60 million bushels of corn a year, mostly off smallholders' land. The feudal privilege was abolished in Queen Elizabeth's reign and the 16th and 17th centuries saw a great boom in the building of dovecotes. Restrictions, however, still existed and these had the backing of reformers supporting the poorer peasants, who continued to lose much of their crops to the wealthy men's birds. We shall find an excellent example of a 17th-century dovecote higher up river at Kelmscott.

The mile from Northmoor Lock to the footbridge now spanning the river at the site of the former HART'S WEIR contains the very soul of the stripling Thames. It is quite undramatic but so peaceful, so far-away-from-it-all, so cosily benign and green, especially in the misty, dew-soaked hours that promise a genial summer day, that it epitomizes the best of England—that landscape which, though rarely grand, is preferable to any other in the world. It is not, as we generally suppose, a natural phenomenon but artificial and man-made. And it is man-made in two ways. First in the physical sense through planting, hedging, farming, draining, building and so on; secondly in a mental sense. We appreciate it—we *make* it in our minds' eyes—because poets and painters have taught us to look at it in certain ways which we might otherwise not have seen. Negley Farson, the American writer, expresses the same idea in his novel, *Sons of Noah:*

Here I would like to stress the influence of the scenes we were talking about. In this there lay a difference between the American and the Old World conversational background. In Europe, for instance, the pleasure of the senses in viewing something is largely the result of book-learning: the pleasure in viewing old cathedrals, paintings, historic towns—knowing their story—only in Switzerland (if you can forget the tourists) does Nature itself grip you to the exclusion of everything else—to the *exclusion* of every other thought—*even in the English countryside it is the poetry of the English which gives you the fullest enjoyment of it* . . . (The italics are this author's).

On the left near the footbridge you can just see the thatched roof of an old cottage which must at one time have been the home of the weir-keeper, for, though the old flash lock has gone, the spot is still known as Hart's Weir (that fertile family again) or Rudge's Weir. The place is associated with the true love story of Weir-keeper Rudge's daughter, Betty, and a certain peer of the realm. To Bablock Hythe one sunny day to fish came young William Flower, second Viscount Ashbrook, then an undergraduate at Christ Church. Here he found sweet Betty helping her father at the ferry. It was love at first sight. Before long the young milord removed Betty from her cottage, not in the manner of Henry Rex to a bower at the end of a maze, but to a nearby family of gentlefolk to be fitted for a higher kind of life than that to which she was accustomed. The pair were married in Northmoor Church in 1766 and in the register you can still see their signatures. The union, which produced two boys and four girls, seems to have been an unusually happy one, although it did not last so very long. William died eighteen years after meeting his Betty and then she, having born ten years of widowhood, married again, this time a brilliant theological scholar, one Dr. John Jones of Jesus College, Oxford. She herself died, 'a courtly old grandame', in 1808. One of her grand-daughters married the sixth Duke of Marlborough and through her the humble blood of the Rudges has enriched that of other aristocratic families.

The Rudges, or Ridges, like the Harts, have long associations with the Thames, though the last of the family in the service of the Thames Conservancy retired nearly fifty years ago. His daughters were renowned for their beauty, but it seems that neither had the good fortune of their relative to marry a wealthy peer—a prerogative held in their day almost exclusively by the ladies of the Gaiety chorus.

Another mile and a quarter brings us to NEW BRIDGE, which is generally supposed to be the oldest on the river. It is more likely, however, that the three-arched Radcot Bridge has the oldest existing bridge foundation, New Bridge being called so because it followed Radcot. Erected about 1250, but largely rebuilt in the middle of the 15th century, New Bridge has considerable charm and character with its old stonework, its pointed and groined arches and its projecting piers which act not only as cutwaters but, carried up to parapet level, form accommodating recesses for pedestrians. Cromwell's forces captured the bridge during the Civil War in 1644 and this forced the King, who was established at Oxford, to retreat northwards. An inn stands at either end. That in Oxfordshire, the *Rose Revived* is the larger and now a rebuilt, modern hotel rather than an ancient tavern but well conceived in Cotswold stone. Just above the bridge on the right, the River Windrush flows in.

Soon we pass the hamlet of SHIFFORD (meaning Sheep Ford) which stands in Oxfordshire, a stone's throw away from the river. It is of no account today but it is historically important because here in 885 Alfred the Great held the first Parliament, the Mother of Parliaments—about the same time that he is supposed to have founded the University of Oxford. An old manuscript tells us that: 'There sate, at Sifford, many Thanes, many Bishops, and many learned men, also Earls and awful Knights. There was Earl Elfric, very learned in the law; and Alfred, England's herdsman—England's darling. He was King in England: he taught them that could hear him, how they should live.' Centuries ago Shifford was, according to tradition, an important town and a Royal Borough with sixteen churches and many inns. Now it consists of a farm, a few cottages and one tiny church of 1863, on whose site Alfred is believed to have erected a thanksgiving memorial.

Though Shifford itself is very old, the lock just above it is the youngest on the river, for it was not opened until 1898, the cut being engineered from an old side channel. This is the most remote and inaccessible of all Thames locks and that is exactly the feeling you get when you moor up the side of the cut above the lock, or along the short but lovely weir stream. This is just the place to rest and do absolutely nothing in complete contentment. But if you feel restless let us go along now and past the farm at CHIMNEY down the Oxfordshire lane to visit Cote and Bampton.

COTE, or Coate (meaning a sheepfold) is distinguished for its grand Stuart manor house of stone. Originally this was Elizabethan with an E plan but only a small part of this remains. Here Charles I, when he was fleeing from his enemies after a local reverse, probably the Battle of Newbridge, once sought succour and shelter. In its garden walls running by the lane are inset some wrought iron gates of pleasing design bearing the date 1704 and known as the Blenheim Gates, for they were erected to commemorate the famous battle.

Another interesting building in Cote is the Baptist Chapel, one of the earliest existing examples of its sort in the country, built in 1756. It is, of course, very plain and simple having a square plan, an internal gallery running round three sides and a central table pew. The Baptist community still flourishing at Cote may be the oldest Protestant church in the kingdom because its history can be traced back to the days of Wycliffe's unauthorised Poore Preachers, those Lollards who came from Oxford with their first fervent words and the manuscripts of their newly translated bible to read and preach in the Oxfordshire and Berkshire villages, notably here at Cote and in nearby Longworth below the great market cross.

The district around was also the centre of the Civil War which brought a twenty years' rest to the puritan meetings. Edgehill is only twenty miles away and Newbury only about twenty-five. Battles took place at Radcot and Newbridge, at Faringdon, Bampton and Standlake, while at Tenfoot Bridge, a short way up river, a violent skirmish was fought.

BAMPTON, or to give the full title Bampton-in-the-Bush, lies two miles west of Cote. The name is probably derived from the Saxon *beam*, a tree, and *tun*, an enclosure. It is now little more than a large village but was once a prosperous and important town, renowned for its markets, especially its Horse Fair, and for its industry of fellmongering, the making of leather and sheepskin breeches and jerkins worn by labouring men. Fellmongering in the old way is now a dead craft, but the tradition of Morris dancing still goes on here with unabated vigour each Whit Monday of the year. Then two teams perform rhythmically along by the buff stone cottages, dressed all in white with coloured ribbons and streamers and with jingling bell-pads on their legs, while accompanying the colourful dancers go a fiddler, a sword bearer and a Fool wielding a bladder.

Bampton Church is a beauty and has a remarkably fine octagonal 13th-century spire with belfry windows and four projecting statues, which acts as a landmark for many miles around. The church contains examples of every style from the 11th to the 18th century. The interior with its transepts gives a noble, spatial effect and has many interesting details. Note, for instance, the 14th-century reredos cut from one piece of stone, the graceful cinquefoil inner frames to the windows, and, carved in the stonework of one of the piers near the south transept, a mass of Crusader Crosses, each about three inches high and similar to those which can still be seen on a wall in Jerusalem. And examine the four 17th-century wall monuments in the vestry with their splendid, flamboyant, baroque sculpture.

On the west of the church is an Elizabethan house called The Deanery, for it was formerly the residence of the Deans of Exeter who still hold the right of presentation to the living. There are some other good houses in the place, several of the Georgian period.

On our way up river once more we emerge from Shifford Cut to see on our left the Golden Ridge of the Berkshire Downs, on whose slope we can just make out the façade of BUCKLAND HOUSE. This was designed, it is believed, by John Wood of Bath, the Younger, who completed some of his father's work at Bath and there carried out on his own the famous Royal Crescent. Buckland House was built in stone about 1760 and is composed of a formal classical central block connected to two balancing octagonal pavilions by vaulted passages. The huge recessed addition behind the central block was added early in the 20th century, a competent enlargement by W. Romaine-Walker. The village at Buckland is pretty and has a good cruciform church.

Ahead to the left of us now we can see FARINGDON CLUMP with its great, tall tower, a modern folly erected in 1936 by the fourteenth Lord Berners to designs by the eighth Duke of Wellington. From the top, they say, magnificent views can be had in all directions. The folly forms a prominent landmark in this part of the Vale of the White Horse and will be in sight from the river for many miles.

Soon we pass under TENFOOT BRIDGE, another of those simple, satisfying timber structures of the river. Thacker suggests that the curious name derives from a weir which once stood here having a ten-foot-wide flash-opening for boats. After two miles of uneventful, open country we reach TADPOLE BRIDGE and the *Trout Inn*. The bridge is a good stone design of 1802; it has a single wide arch for the river is narrow here.

A mile on lies RUSHEY LOCK with a square cottage which is very pleasing, even though it was built in 1896. So on through Radcot Lock to the smaller of the two RADCOT BRIDGES, marked for many miles around by two stupendous lombardy poplars. This is the new bridge built in 1787 when the present navigational cut was dug in anticipation of an increase in traffic from the Thames and Severn Canal. The old, now disused, channel runs a short distance away on the left below the other Radcot Bridge, almost certainly the oldest existing bridge on the river. This is curious in other ways. It has three arches, the two outer ones being pointed and the centre one being more or less rounded. There exists a tradition that the centre arch was originally also pointed but that it was knocked down during a battle which took place here in 1387 during the reign of Richard II, when the forces of Robert de Vere, the King's Minister and Duke of Ireland, were defeated by those of the barons under Bolingbroke. Afterwards the bridge was repaired with the present round arch. But this is another of those tales 'for the truth of which I cannot vouch'. Over this centre arch is the socket for a cross, relic of the days when bridges were regarded as sacred structures maintained, with the roads, as a sacred duty by the medieval religious houses. The socket was used for baptisms until quite recent times.

From Radcot, Burford stone for the building of St. Paul's Cathedral was loaded onto rafts and floated down to London and for many years this was a wharfage centre for supplying coal for the towns and villages of the district.

FARINGDON lies some three miles away in Berkshire and if you do not fancy the walk you can take a bus there from Radcot. It is a small market town of stone, the only stone town in Berkshire, though, in truth, it contains much brickwork too. It has much character and a long history—a royal residence in Saxon times, later presented by King John to the monks of Beaulieu Abbey in Hampshire, held by the Royalists in the Civil War, and the town of *Tom Brown's Schooldays*.

The church, which is cruciform, has a low tower over the crossing and seems to miss its spire which was destroyed by Cromwell's artillery and never replaced. One enters by the south door, which is decorated with some good 13th-century wrought ironwork still in splendid condition, and then one is struck at once by that fascinating sense, often to be felt in cruciform churches and here strengthened by a generous chancel, that space itself has become good form—a sense of a 'landscaped' interior in which movement is an exciting adventure of exploration. The general effect is here improved by the four grand piers of clustered columns supporting the tower.

The interior is remarkable also for its several fine monuments, the most notable being the early 17th-century alabaster effigy of Dorothy, Lady Unton, who kneels in the north transept. Her husband, Sir Henry Unton, knighted for gallantry at the

O

terrible massacre of Zutphen and twice sent as Queen Elizabeth's ambassador to France, has a wall monument hanging behind his lady with a beautiful carving in white marble at its base of a winged angel's head and a skull.

North of the chancel is the Pye chapel with various monuments to that local family, whose most distinguished member was Henry James Pye, poet laureate to George III. He it was who once wrote an ode about birds which led to the composition of *Sing a Song of Sixpence*, the nursery rhyme with its reference to blackbird 'pie'. Otherwise he seems only to have been remembered in Byron's line:

> Better to err with Pope, than shine with Pye.

This Pye built Faringdon House, which lies north of the church, home of the late Lord Berners. Completed in about 1780 it was designed, like Buckland House, by the younger Wood of Bath in the same refined, formal, classical manner, though here the wings are merely blank, curving walls. Tucked away among the trees behind the church this perfect and unspoiled example of a gentleman's small country seat of the 18th century unfortunately cannot be seen except from the grounds.

After Radcot comes GRAFTON LOCK and then we soon pass the Berkshire hamlet of EATON HASTINGS with its farmhouse and its old church with stone slated roof, wherein we could see, if we wished, a Jacobean pulpit and two stained glass windows by Sir Edward Burne-Jones, the Pre-Raphaelite painter. The country is mostly flat around here and is lavishly sprinkled with concrete pill boxes as though the people were still expecting a local attack by the whole German army. There on our right lies Kelmscott and having been refreshed at the ANCHOR INN, which lies by the spot where the last of the flash locks stood right up to 1938, we cross the footbridge into Oxfordshire to visit one of the major sights of our journey.

KELMSCOTT MANOR has become famous because in 1871 William Morris, poet, reformer, reviver of handicrafts, and leading light in that strange, loosely knit band of aesthetes known as the Pre-Raphaelite Brotherhood, bought the place as a holiday retreat for his family and shared it for a while with Dante Gabriel Rossetti. It was left by Morris's daughter, May, to Oxford University as a home of rest for learned men but it is so remotely situated that no learned men came. Now it is leased as a home to a lady who was a close friend of the late May Morris, on condition that she permits visitors who are interested to look round the place. Thus, in a vague and typically English way, the house is now a national monument to one of our famous men while yet retaining the intimacy of a private home.

Inside can be seen many Pre-Raphaelite relics—pieces of well-made furniture designed by Philip Webb, Morris tapestries and wall-papers, an exquisite sketch of a recumbent Mrs. Morris by Rossetti, two crayon heads, also by him, of the young Morris daughters—Mary, called May, sweet and gentle, and Jane, petulant and wild.

The gabled house is difficult to date exactly but, though it has a satisfactory unity, it is almost certainly of two different periods. A figure cut in a rafter looks like 1571 but may be 1511, and suggests that the earlier part is Elizabethan. The later part is obviously early Jacobean. Though called a manor, it has always lacked manorial rights and belonged for many years to the Turners, a family of yeoman farmers. At the time of the Commonwealth it is said that the house came into the owner-ship of one of the Roundhead leaders who signed Charles's death warrant. The walls of well-laid rubble have a slight and subtle batter which gives a feeling of strength and relieves the somewhat stern character of the place. The attics are specially impressive with their sturdy, strutted roof frames of oak and elm.

Morris was passionately attached to Kelmscott Manor, which he has vividly described in *The Quest* and in *News from Nowhere*. Seeing it now in its walled garden where the holly-hocks cluster, the wide meadow behind and the great elm trees swaying around, how well we can understand why he wrote of it so lovingly: 'It has come to be to me the type of the pleasant places of the earth . . . As others love the race of man through their lovers or their children, so I love the earth through that small space of it.'

In the old stone KELMSCOTT VILLAGE are two buildings worth an inspection. The first is the 17th-century dovecote in the yard of the Manor Farm, whose interior is dramatic with limewashed walls pierced with a regular pattern of black nesting holes. The second is the small church in whose churchyard the Morris family lies buried beneath a simple stone monument chastely lettered. The church, mainly transitional Norman, is pleasing and contains a good, Norman tub font, some old glass in its east window and the remains of an early wall painting.

Our next stop is at BUSCOT CHURCH on the Berkshire side. In its churchyard are some handsome, 18th-century carved headstones in the Cotswold style and a memorial to a former Lord Mayor of London, named Nash. Within is an east window of the Good Shepherd by Burne-Jones, a fine, florid, 18th-century Italian lectern and a pulpit graced with three delicate paintings in panels representing the Adoration of the Three Kings, the Annunciation, and the Virgin and Child, believed by a former rector to be a triptych painted by Andrea Mantegna. General opinion, however, is that they were painted by Mabuse *alias* Jan Gossaert, a Fleming who came as a young man early in the 16th century to England, where he was well received at court. The pulpit with its beautiful paintings was presented to the church in 1908 and in its refined sophistication seems, like the lectern, to be oddly out of place in this old English church, yet for itself is worth coming quite a long way to see. It is believed that the carpets and curtains in the church were designed by William Morris.

The rectory standing near the church is a large and noble stone building of the late 17th century with a coved cornice and a series of decorative wrought iron brackets supporting the rainwater pipes. Its complex stone roof slopes look especially attractive from the river.

BUSCOT VILLAGE lies some distance away from the church and is of interest as a model settlement laid out in 1879 with stone cottages, a village well and parish hall—the whole being a solid job with atmosphere and feeling.

BUSCOT HOUSE, which in its turn, lies a mile or so beyond the village was built about 1780 with some additions, including gate lodges, of 1930. It stands in a pleasant park with a lake but is not outstanding as a building. Inside is a room decorated by Burne-Jones with painted panels, set in Adam-style surroundings, commissioned by the first Lord Faringdon, a patron of the Pre-Raphaelites; hence the Burne-Jones windows in the churches of Buscot and Eaton Hastings. The house is open to the public at certain times, for the present Lord Faringdon has presented the property to the National Trust.

We may have to work BUSCOT LOCK ourselves, because though it is nominally under the lock-keeper at St. John's, he may not be available to turn the paddles for us. Then after a winding mile we reach ST. JOHN'S BRIDGE and LOCK—the last and highest lock on the river. The bridge is of no account as architecture, being mainly a 19th-century reconstruction, but it stands on the site of one of the three earliest bridges of the Thames; this was built in the 13th century after those of London and Radcot. Just by the bridge on the Gloucestershire side (for Oxfordshire ended just above Kelmscott) is the old *Trout Inn* which was called until 1704 St. John Baptist's Head on account of a hospital which stood here of that name founded in 1220. Such hospitals, organised and run by the Church, existed in most towns in the Middle Ages and to a large extent succoured the poor at a time when no Poor Laws had been formulated. They took in the old and the sick, gave hospitality to impecunious travellers and attended to lepers and lunatics. Later on the hospital here, from which the bridge takes its name, was expanded to become a priory of Black Monks, but this was dissolved some time before the Reformation. During the 18th century the outer walls of this priory were still intact and within them the Lechlade overseers had built a workhouse which, in the way of those days, had been farmed out as a business. Report says that the interior was divided into stalls, like horse boxes, in which the pauper women sat spinning, encouraged by the master with violence and abuse. This cruel and unsavoury place disappeared after the erection of the Pest Houses in 1795. You can still see the remains of the foundations of the priory, and its well and fishpond, if you apply at a bungalow bearing the name St. John's Priory.

Ahead of us now we can see across a half-mile of grazing land the roofs of LECHLADE and rising above them the spire of Lechlade Church, 'a pratie pyramis of stone' as Leland saw it. Soon we are moored by Lechlade's charming bridge. This was built to replace a ferry in 1792, three years after the opening of the Thames and Severn Canal and the building of the Lechlade Wharf. The bridge is called Halfpenny Bridge because of the pedestrian toll of that amount charged for crossing here until 1839. The toll house still stands on the Gloucestershire side. To the east of the bridge is a wide field known as North Meadow, which was once divided in the manner of the ancient strip system of farming used before the Enclosures Acts revolutionized our agriculture. Some of the old boundary stones marking the strips can still be seen.

Lechlade (from the River Lech which unlades itself into the river here) is, as Leland rightly remarks, 'a praty old toune'—a small market centre deriving a fascination partly from its picturesque buildings and partly from its general lay-out and street vistas. Through the village runs a wide main road, for this was for many centuries an important thoroughfare to the western counties. Right back in 1698 a stage coach ran through here to London. This road turns sharply where it widens out to form a market place in front of the old coaching house, the 18th-century *New Inn,* and, nestling here in the corner, rises the beautiful late-Gothic church to form a dominant focus in the village composition.

Lechlade has been an important marketing centre for many centuries, partly because the river brought much commercial traffic. Cheese, and later coal, were commodities handled in a big way and a manuscript of 1692 informs us that 'here comes from Severn and Avon handled at Tewsbery where both these Rivers do unite and elsewhere, on horses and in Carts & Wagons by land great weights of Cheese especially that sort gos by y name of Cheshire Cheese, for hereabout The Boates Masters have warehouses to secure their goods; and Hoys in time of scarcity, & other goods comes from London-ward hether & are sent as aforesaid by land to Severn and thence in Boats to Bristol and elswere, & in ships to Ireland.'

That was before the Thames and Severn Canal was opened, and in 1793, some years after that event, a Lechlade bargemaster states that the chief goods he carried to London were 'Iron, Copper, Tin, manufactured and pig Iron, Brass, Spelter, Cannon, Cheese, Nails, all Iron goods and Bomb Shells.' He would return with 'groceries, Deals, Foreign Timber, Merchandise of every Kind, a few Coals, and of late Raw Hides for Tewkesbury and Worcester and Gun-powder to Bristol and Liverpool.' Cther goods carried would have been salt from

Cheshire, Taynton stone and coal from Avonmouth and the Forest of Dean.

The church was built as a whole in the reign of Edward IV about 1470 in the early Perpendicular style. Apart from its splendid spire, its exterior is notable for its magnificently carved gargoyles. The best of the simple interior is the effect produced by the east end of the nave. The nave runs into the chancel, both being of the same width, but the junction of the two is strongly articulated by a pointed arch which is exactly like the arches running towards it between nave and aisles. Then at each side of the chancel arch and closing the east ends of the aisles spring smaller arches. This produces the impression of transepts. Good details to notice inside are the carved and painted wooden roof bosses in the chancel ceiling and the brass candelabrum of 1730 which hangs in the centre of the nave.

Lechlade has many old houses, two of the best being Church House, a 17th-century stone building entered from the church-yard east of the church, and one of rather later date of brick-work, with stone quoins and an unusual entrance canopy, standing at the bend in Sherborne Street. At one corner of its front garden stands a square gazebo, an example of a type of small building which is a Lechlade speciality, for there are at least six in, or near, the town. The best and most elaborate of these stands at the entrance to Butler's Court Farm on the Fair-ford Road, and has stone walls, stone roof and chimney and Georgian sash windows. The purpose of these little structures was to serve both as a waiting room for stage coach passengers and as a lookout from which to observe the people and the carriages passing by.

In Sherborne Street is another of those formal, austere but characterful Baptist Chapels, this example dating from 1817.

At Lechlade we are almost at the end of our journey by water, though even in the low level of summer it is possible, with some effort, to work a punt or a canoe up to Cricklade, eleven miles away. Most river craft can certainly navigate to Inglesham, a hamlet lying about a mile above Lechlade on the Wiltshire side. On the way there we pass the entrances to the River Coln and to the THAMES AND SEVERN CANAL. Ever since the time of Charles II schemes had been proposed for uniting the two principal rivers of the kingdom, an idea which had continually occupied many minds—Alexander Pope's for one. He describes his poet's vision of a new Cotswold waterway in a letter of 1722 in this way:

I could pass whole days in only describing the future, and as yet visionary, beauties that are to rise in those scenes (in Lord Bathurst's woods at Cirencester), the palace that is to be built, the pavilions that are to glitter, the colonnades that are to adorn them; nay more, the meeting of the Thames and Severn, which (when the noble owner has finer dreams than ordinary) are to be led into each others embraces, through secret caverns of not above twelve or fifteen miles, till they rise and celebrate their marriage in the midst of an immense amphitheatre, which is to be the admiration of posterity a hundred years hence.

But it was not until 1789 that the 30-mile project was realised, having taken less than seven years and more than £200,000 to complete. Its opening was a great occasion. As reported in the *Gentleman's Magazine* of November 19 of that year:

A boat, with the union flag at her masthead, passed laden for the first time to St. John's Bridge, below Lechlade, in the presence of great numbers of people, who answered a salute of twelve pieces of cannon from Buscott Park by loud huzzas. A dinner was given at five of the principal inns at Lechlade, and the day ended with ringing of bells, a bonfire, and a ball.

In spite of this jubilant start, the canal was never very successful. It has been virtually derelict since the turn of the century and today it is impassable, being quite dried out for much of its length. Temple Thurston must have been one of the last to navigate the canal and in *The Flower of Gloster* he describes the journey he made upon it in 1911, and the beauties of the Golden Valley through which he passed. If you fancy a country tramp in peaceful solitude there could be no better way to choose than the tow-path of this dead waterway. It will give you an opportunity to inspect that great engineering feat, the Sapperton Tunnel, which passes for two and a half miles through the great ridge dividing the two river basins—the second longest canal tunnel in England.

A charming group of buildings marks the entrance to the canal—a low, timber footbridge, a cottage which retains the iron eyes in the roof beams to which the barge horses were tethered when the cottage was a stable, and a curious round house like a Martello tower, once a canal employee's dwelling and one of a standard type unique to this canal. Added to this complex is one of those small, delightful canal bridges of stone, a tumble-down lock and a background of poplars and willow trees.

A short way beyond on the Wiltshire side, half-hidden behind foliage, stands the little church of INGLESHAM, once the chapel of a priory. Built in the 11th century, it is rough, simple and rich in spirit with its bell turret and, close by, its unusually perfect fifteen-foot stone cross. The inside is filled with old box pews and a wall bears a lettered plaque of copper stating that: 'This Church was repaired in 1888-9 through the energy and with the help of William Morris who loved it.' Unlike so many restorers of his time, Morris has done no harm here and the place still holds all its ancient atmosphere. The most beautiful object in the church is the stone carving of the madonna and child inserted near a corner of the south wall. This is believed to be of the 13th century and to have been brought here from the Priory of St. John Baptist when that place was dissolved. It possesses the fine, worn patina of its age but its bold and simple form renders it quite modern in effect; it might almost be a work by Epstein.

Now the river changes its character again. It is a mere stream six or seven yards across. The riverside houses, the busy locks and the broad waters of the earlier reaches seem very far away. The towpath ended at Lechlade and now the fertile fields with their grazing cattle, wild flowers, hawthorn hedges and pollard willows come right down to the water on either hand. For many miles we may not see a soul. The bucolic peace is absolute. As Boydell wrote:

The pasturage that borders the Isis, during its course through North Wilts, is exceedingly rich and has given rise to the adage, 'That an ox left to himself, would, of all England, choose to live in the north of Wiltshire.' ... This part of the country was also formerly thought, from its fecundity, to be more favoured by God's presence than any other; it had, likewise, more mitred abbeys and sacred edifices than any other two shires, whence arose the ancient proverb of, 'As sure as God's in Gloucestershire.'

On the way to Cricklade we shall pass a few sleepy villages. The first is KEMPSFORD having a manor house with a history

Bell Tower, Castle Eaton

older than the Conquest, fragments of a castle and a fine church, 'very ancient and capacious', as Cobbett found it on one of his rides. It is mainly of the 14th century with a great buttressed tower, a curiously, long, tall nave and a number of interesting details including a painted vault below the tower, some old glass, a timber roof and some early tiling.

The second village we come to is CASTLE EATON, long ago a place of size and strength. Its church has an interesting Sanctus Bell turret built entirely of thick stone slabs and retaining its original bell. A Sanctus Bell, by the way, is one which was always rung out when the priest came to that part of the service: *Sanctus, Sanctus, Dominus Deus Sábaoth,* so that those who could not come to church might understand what a solemn office the congregation were at that moment engaged in and be moved 'to lift up their hearts to Him that made them'.

CRICKLADE is now a small country town but it has an important history going back at least to Roman times, for Ermine Street crosses the river here. St. Augustine may have seen it; here Alfred the Great forded over in about the year 878 during his war with Guthrum; over a century later, in 1016, as the

Saxon Chronicle recalls, 'Came King Cnut with a marine force of one hundred and sixty ships, and ealdorman Edric with him over the Thames at Cricklade', from where they went up into Warwickshire burning, harrying and pillaging, 'as their way is'. In his *Sweet Thames Run Softly* Robert Gibbings makes the sensible suggestion that, since the river is so shallow here, these 'ships' were not sea-going craft but bodies of men, rather less than a hundred each in number and equal to a ship's complement. Legend says that Cricklade possessed a seat of learning as far back as the 7th century, that is before the University of Oxford was founded.

The town has two churches. That of St. Mary is small and has a good Norman chancel arch and a Jacobean pulpit. That of St. Sampson is larger, and, though its body is mainly early Gothic, its massive tower is very late Gothic of about 1550, built at the time of the Wool Churches. The clumsy pinnacles render the tower far too heavy and out of scale with the building as a whole and the detail is emasculated, but, seen from far off dominating the landscape above the trees, it is noble and dramatic.

Now at last we must abandon any sort of craft and, to reach the river's source still some ten miles further on, we shall have to take to our feet. At ASHTON KEYNES four miles beyond Cricklade, this 'far-off, lonely mother of the Thames' is but nine feet wide and trickles below a row of some twenty little bridges of stone, brick or wood, which give access from the lane to the cottages and houses on the other side. Though the design of many of the bridges is undistinguished, the general effect is attractive. To this small village in 1826 Cobbett came riding and remarked that 'to a certainty it has been a large market town; and such numerous lanes crossing and cutting the land into such little bits that it must have been a large town. A very curious place.'

At SOMERFORD KEYNES we shall have difficulty in finding the course of the river, for here in summer time the pebbles of its bed are completely dry.

And so to the very source. But where is it? The question has been argued about and about for centuries. Some say it is at the Seven Springs three miles from Cheltenham; others that it is at the Thames Head which lies further west near Cirencester.

At Seven Springs you will find a little, neglected pool formed by the springs and a stone tablet above it inscribed in Latin *Hic Tuus O Tamisine Pater Septemgeminus Fons.* But when the rains come the springs pour forth to feed the Churn, and the Churn is not the Thames but a tributary which joins the river at Cricklade. Therefore it is now agreed by most that the Thames begins at THAMES HEAD. This is situated a mile or so away from the village of Kemble near the Fosse Way in a lonely field called Trewsbury Mead. Just near the spot runs the dried-up bed of the Thames and Severn Canal and beyond that rises the mound of a Roman camp called Trewsbury Castle. On the bole of a tree in this Trewsbury Mead are carved the initials T H. Of the source itself, just below the tree, you will see in the summer only a slight dip in the ground surrounded by a few loose stones. There is not a drop of water near but here in winter a small spring bubbles up. Formerly quite a large well existed at this spot and Boydell both depicts it and describes it as 'enclosed within a circular wall of stone raised eight feet from the surface of the meadow'—the very place where perhaps two thousand years ago Roman legionaries encamped at Trewsbury Castle came to fill their ewers.

Although it must be conceded that Seven Springs lies some fifteen miles beyond Thames Head and so provides the highest source of Thames water and the furthest from the sea, we will concur with Leland that 'Isis riseth at 3 myles from Cirencestre, not far from a village called Kemble, within half a mile of the fosseway, wher the very hed of Isis ys.' We have reached the beginning and—

THE END

Index

Note: Italic figures indicate illustrations

INDEX

INDEX